Asianfail

THE ASIAN AMERICAN EXPERIENCE

Series Editors
Eiichiro Azuma
Jigna Desai
Martin F. Manalansan IV
Lisa Sun-Hee Park
David K. Yoo

Roger Daniels, Founding Series Editor

A list of books in the series appears at the end of this book.

Asianfail

Narratives of Disenchantment and the Model Minority

ELEANOR TY

**UNIVERSITY OF
ILLINOIS PRESS**
Urbana, Chicago, and Springfield

The University of Illinois Press gratefully acknowledges
financial assistance provided by Wilfrid Laurier
University Office of Research Services for the
publication of this book.
1 2 3 4 5 C P 5 4 3 2 1
♾ This book is printed on acid-free paper.

Library of Congress Control Number: 2016958953
ISBN 978-0-252-04088-7 (hardcover)
ISBN 978-0-252-08235-1 (paperback)
ISBN 978-0-252-09938-0 (e-book)

Contents

Illustrations

Acknowledgments

I thank my colleagues and students in the Department of English and Film Studies at Wilfrid Laurier University for their friendship and for providing a stimulating teaching and working environment. Thanks are due to the Research Office and the Vice-President: Academic for encouraging my project with course releases and with the University Research Professor award in 2015. The project was initially funded by a grant from the Social Sciences and Humanities Research Council of Canada.

For lively and thought-provoking conversations about reading and teaching Asian North American and graphic narratives, I am grateful to Monica Chiu, Patricia Chu, Rocío Davis, Don Goellnicht, Y-Dang Troeung, Julie Rak, Thy Phu, and members of the Toronto Pacific Exchange reading group. It was a pleasure to work with intelligent and efficient editors at the University of Illinois Press, especially Dawn Durante and Jennifer L. Comeau. And thank you to my family members, David, Jason and his wife Clare, Jeremy, and Miranda Hunter, for their continuing love and patience.

Parts of chapter 3 were originally published as "Little Daily Miracles: Global Desires, Haunted Memories, and Modern Technologies in Madeleine Thien's *Certainty*" in *Moving Migration: Narrative Transformations in Asian American Literature*, edited by Johanna C. Kardux and Doris Einsiedel (Berlin: LIT Verlag, 2010), 45–60.

Parts of chapters 4 and 5 were originally published as "Affect, Family, and the Past in Two Plays by Catherine Hernandez" in *Asian Canadian Theatre*, edited by Nina Lee Aquino and Ric Knowles (Toronto: Playwrights Canada Press, 2011), 212–22.

Asianfail

Introduction

The hashtags #Asian Fail, #failasian, and #Asianfailure on Tumblr, Instagram, and Twitter feature tweets, pictures, and anecdotes of Asians who "fail" at doing what Asians are supposed to be good at. Asians make insider jokes about their own inability to pick up food with chopsticks, to cook rice, or to shine at math and computers. Many of these posts are funny, riffing on cultural stereotypes of Asians who are supposed to excel at playing the violin or who are so nerdy that they have no social or sex life. Some examples:

FailAsian, July 7, 2011: "I only got an A instead of an A+"
@Asian_Failure, September 2, 2011: 30% of Chinese adults live with their
    parents

FIGURE 1. High-expectation Asian father on Spelling B meme

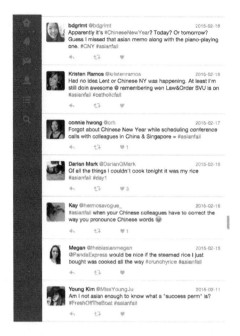

FIGURE 2. #Asianfail examples from Twitter, February 2015

Jenny C.: "being destroyed in badminton" failAsian
July 22, 2011, High Expectations Asian Father: "You got B+ on blood test? Failure runs through veins."

The U.S. Context: Model Minority Discourse

The more serious side of this phenomenon of high expectations of Asian subjects in North America has been referred to as the problem of the "model minority," especially in the United States. Since the 1960s, Asian Americans have been used as examples in contrast to other minority groups, such as blacks and later Latinos, who were perceived to be less successful in schools and in their professions (see Osajima 215ff.). An oft-cited 1966 article in *U.S. News and World Report* praised Asian Americans for discipline, low crime rates, a willingness to work hard, and strong family values. Besides presenting the questionable view of America as the "land of opportunity" for individuals who worked hard (Osajima 217), the article reinforced stereotypes about Asians and the myth of the model minority, entrenching some problematic assumptions that would last for the next couple of decades. As Keith Osajima explains, "Asian American success constituted a direct critique of Blacks who sought relief through federally supported social programs. . . . The achievements of Asians diffused the black militants' claim that America was fundamentally a racist society, structured to keep minorities in a subordinate position. The Asian American experience identified cultural values and hard work as the keys to success"(217). One critical issue was the blunt use of race, which, as Tomo Hattori notes, "functions as the general equivalent, as the standard measure that makes human bodies and racial culture commensurable and equal to each other," resulting in a "flattening of human diversity into racial fact" (230). Sze Wei Ang also notes the paradoxical use of race: "the myth of the model minority allows critics to dismiss the fact that race plays a part in socio-economic processes, but even then, the myth continues to depend upon race for its very construction. Historical materialist critiques of this myth furthermore identify it as a function of capitalist ideology that tries to protect private property rights at the expense of state policies, such as affirmative action" (121–22).

Scholars have questioned the kind of success model minority discourse lauds, as it is seen as the "(re)production of representations of the successful formation of a particularly constructed Asian American subjectivity" (Palumbo-Liu, *Asian/American* 396). Remarking on the popularity of novels such as *The Woman Warrior*, *The Joy Luck Club*, *Typical American*, and *China Boy* in the 1990s, David Palumbo-Liu argues that "in model minority discourse we find the instantiation of a collective psychic identification that constructs a very specific concept of the negotiations between social trauma and private health" (*Asian/American* 398). Happiness is promised to those who subscribe to "hegemonic ideologies" (398) that promote the "work ethic of self-affirmative action" or the attainment of "upward mobility on the strength of inner conviction and self-help" (399). Like self-affirmative action, model minority discourse assumes that individuals can transcend specific historical and material conditions in order to achieve happiness. The need for structural change, for governmental support of programs that enable minority groups to gain equal access to privileges usually accorded to dominant groups, is thus elided. Palumbo-Liu notes that popular Asian American narratives animate the "expected themes of subject-split, cultural alienation and confusion, and coming-to-terms that fits the stereotypical image of the model minority" (410). This type of literature "of an assimilated group now at peace after a 'phase' of adjustment is dangerous in its powerful closing-off of a multiplicity of real, lived, social contradictions and complexities that stand outside (or at least significantly complicate) the formula of the highly individuated 'identity crisis'" (410). Similarly, Victor Bascara criticizes model minority discourse and argues that critique of the model minority stereotype can be understood as a critique of U.S. imperialism: "The model-minority myth has functioned as a way of reading progressive historical change. That is, the present has reckoned with uncomfortable pasts and is doing right by the wronged by incorporating them, or more precisely, by allowing a putatively color-blind and gender-neutral market to sort things out. The resulting vision is the smooth and compliant incorporation of Asian difference into American civilization" (2).

The Canadian Context: Visible Minorities

In Canada, the term *model minority* does not have the same resonance in the media or public discourse as in the United States. Asian Canadians, including those from East Asia, Southeast Asia, and South Asia, are part of the group officially designated as *visible minorities*, a category of people who are non-Caucasian in race and nonwhite in color and who are not Aboriginal. Since Pierre Trudeau's government in the 1970s, the term *visible minority* has been used by Statistics Canada, Immigration Canada, the Employment Equity Act, and other government offices to classify people and provide data about population, immigrants, workplaces, diversity, and more recently market trends. For example, a report released by Statistics Canada in 2011 revealed that nearly 6,264,800 people, or 19.1 percent of the Canadian population, identified themselves as visible minorities. The increase from 16.2 percent in 2006 was largely due to new immigrants from non-European countries, such as the Philippines, China, India, and Pakistan, the top-sending countries in the preceding decade. In 2011, the largest visible minority group in Canada was South Asian, followed by Chinese (Statistics Canada, "2011 National Household Survey"). More often than not, the term *visible minority* is used to show differences in employment, education, age, and population between visible and nonvisible minority groups. In an employment report in 2006, the Government of Canada's Labour Program reported that although more visible minorities had a university degree than nonvisible minorities (28 percent vs. 16 percent), the unemployment rates were still higher for visible minorities than for nonvisible minorities (9 percent vs. 6 percent) (Government of Canada Labour Program). Official discourse on visible minorities primarily focuses on inequities and work that still needs to be done, not necessarily praise of the group's achievements.

Interestingly, best-selling or critically acclaimed Asian Canadian literature published in and before the 1990s does not follow the uniform path of cultural alienation, intergenerational conflict, and integration that Palumbo-Liu outlines. To be sure, there are elements of the immigrant story (displacement, desire for assimilation, and struggle) in all the works, but the progress from hyphenated subjectivity, being between Asia and European America, to model minority is not so linear as the path Palumbo-Liu identifies, or else does not manifest itself as the primary concerns of these works. There is no iconic bildungsroman in Canada comparable to Maxine Hong Kingston's *Woman War-

rior, which celebrates the triumph of individual self. Instead, the most widely known "early" Asian Canadian works are Joy Kogawa's *Obasan* (1981), about the effects of internment and dispersal of Japanese Canadians, and Evelyn Lau's *Runaway* (1989), about a Chinese Canadian girl who lives on the street as a prostitute while trying to become a writer. Denise Chong's biographical account of her grandmother, *The Concubine's Children*, though a kind of early twentieth-century immigrant narrative, was less about individual development than it was a family saga and history. Assimilation and success are deferred to the third generation, to the writer and economist Chong herself. Although the protagonists in these works do not follow the usual trajectory of the immigrant narrative, there are nevertheless parental, familial, social, and cultural expectations, such as Confucian-inspired teachings, that influence Asian Canadians.

In a recent sociological study conducted in Toronto, Sangeetha Navaratnam discovered that her fourteen interviewees, South Asian youths between eighteen and twenty-six who had spent the previous ten years in Canada, had never heard the term *model minority* (47). However, they did experience guilt, shame, parental influence, and psychological stresses in their career decisions or educational choices (57–59). Parents preferred professional careers, such as engineering, medicine, and law, over nonprofessional ones, such as social work or teaching. Many immigrant parents have high expectations and want their children to have the kind of future that they themselves could not have. Displacing their own ambitions (and sometimes failures) onto their children, they desire that their children have careers that would make their own sacrifice and hard work worthwhile. With or without the explicit discourse of the model minority myth, Asian Canadians, like Asian Americans, feel a certain amount of pressure to excel and perform. Guofang Li argues that the myth can actually become destructive for underachieving Asian Pacific children, especially those whose first language is not English (70, 73). The myth renders invisible the "diverse and complex experiences of Asian children" (71) and does not reflect "the increased evidence of Asian underachievement, dropout, and socio-economic gap" (72). Even if the term *model minority* is not used overtly, the concept has become transnational, negatively influencing educational practices across North America.

Ethnic Differences among Asian Americans and Asian Canadians

The assumption that they will succeed, whether or not it is overtly conveyed, has created unreasonable expectations for many North American Asians, who have become a more heterogeneous group since the 1980s. After 1975, large waves of immigration from Korea, Vietnam, the Philippines, India, Pakistan, and other

Southeast and South Asian countries changed the composition of the North American Asian communities, which had been mostly Chinese and Japanese through the 1970s. Not all these immigrant groups had the same opportunities, language skills, and education as Chinese and Japanese immigrants, yet they were expected to excel in the same way. Stacey Lee points out that "differences in class, ethnicity, generation and gender create differences in circumstances and opportunities that affect the social and academic experiences of Asian American students," and that aggregate data for Asian Americans hide the fact that "poverty is concentrated in certain ethnic groups" (18). For example, the 2000 U.S. Census data indicate "high rates of educational attainment and low rates of poverty among the South Asian population. By contrast, the 2000 Census reveals high rates of poverty and low levels of educational attainment among the Cambodian and Hmong populations" (Stacey Lee 18). Lee notes that there are also "significant class differences" between ethnicities: "While the communities with large Chinese and South Asian American populations are middle and upper middle class, the communities with large Southeast Asian populations are working class and poor" (19). Similarly, Michael Tayag argues that "the 'model minority' myth has proven detrimental, because it masks the psychosocial and educational needs of many Asian Americans, such that these needs have been systematically neglected at the institutional level" (26).

In Canada, differences between Asian Canadians are also related to ethnicity, period of immigration, gender, and the immigration program through which one entered the country. For example, Japanese Canadians, who made up 0.3 percent of the overall population in Canada in 2006, have the highest full-time earnings for both men and women (Government of Canada Labour Program) because on average they have been in Canada longer than other Asian Canadians. More than half of the Nikkei living in the Greater Vancouver area are prewar immigrants or their descendants (Nikkei National Museum and Cultural Centre). In 2001, 77 percent of Canada's Japanese population was born in Canada, and over 38 percent were of mixed heritage (Statistics Canada, "2011 National Household Survey"). In comparison, Filipinos are relative newcomers to Canada, with the majority (83 percent) having completed their degrees in East and Southeast Asia in 2006. Although Filipinos are more likely to be university educated than the nonvisible minority group, they were more likely to work in semi-skilled (44 percent) and low-skilled (18 percent) occupations in 2006. There are many reasons why Filipino Canadians occupy low-skilled occupations, but one factor is the large number of Filipinos, mostly women, who have recently entered Canada through the Live-In Caregiver program. According to Philip Kelly and colleagues, between 1993 and 2009, 52,493 people, 90 percent of them from the Philippines, landed in Canada under the program. During that same period, 30,028 dependents of live-in caregivers also arrived, constituting 2.1 percent of immigrant landings in Canada (Kelly et al. 5). Because the program's rules require extended separation from one's family, immigrants who have completed the program find it more difficult to reenter the open labor market in Canada (8), while their children, who often reunite with their mothers in their teens after five to six years of separation, experience downward education mobility and take low-paying McJobs (Pratt chap. 1).

The Pressure to Succeed

Scholars have advanced various theories for why Asian North Americans are perceived as hard-working and prone to success. In *The Protestant Ethic and the Spirit of Capitalism*, Rey Chow examines the "ethnicization of labor," through which a "laborer becomes ethnicized because she is commodified in specific ways, because she has to pay for her living by performing certain kinds of work, while these kinds of work, despite being generated from within that society, continue to reduce the one who performs them to the position of the outsider, the ethnic" (34). Developing Max Weber's discussions of the Protestant ethic—the internal discipline of hard work, self-sacrifice, and the deferment of pleasure—and the spirit of capitalism, which entails a "drive toward material gains" (43), Chow notes a link between the Protestant sense of a vocation—the triumph of the "soul"—and ethnic subjects in modern and contemporary times (46–47). The link between economic and professional success and a Protestant sense of a vocation is not limited to ethnic subjects, but since "ethnic labor is frequently underpaid, misappropriated, or unrecognized, the handling of ethnic stories in the United States, in academic fields such as African American studies, Asian American studies, Hispanic studies, and so forth, has conventionally taken the form of a settling of past accounts, a renarrativization of the work that had been contributed by generations of ethnic peoples but was never given due acknowledgment by mainstream society" (35). My study is focused less on past injustices than on the idealization of the Protestant work ethic, particularly for ethnic subjects, and its concomitant notions of success.

In his book *The Children of 1965: On Writing, and Not Writing, as an Asian American*, Min Hyoung Song examines "a generation of writers who have largely been born since the mid-1960s" (8), arguing that though race "continues to organize social experiences, to set limits to cultural expression" (10), these writers are "engaged in actively redefining what it means to be an Asian American" (14). Many of them vacillate "between writing and not writing as an Asian American"

(14). Song uses the term *the children of 1965* to highlight the importance of the 1965 U.S. immigration act, which facilitated the radical increase and change in the population of Asian Americans from mainly laborers and service workers to professionals, managers, and an unseen class of service workers and laborers; from mainly males to slightly more Asian women than men; and to a growing cohort of 1.5- and second-generation children (32–34). The new generation is viewed as childlike, "embodying the many promises and anxieties surrounding the imagination of children in the United States" (38). Examples include the Asian American whiz kid, the Asian adoptee, and the multiracial child, who are all expected to be both like and unlike whites. Song prefers the term *expectation* rather than *stereotype* to describe the pressures on these Asian Americans, noting that "expectations are certainly ascribed, but they also require active identification to be made fully into a set of ideas with material meaning in one's life" (43). He writes, "Expectations might thus be thought of as occupying the spaces in between possibility and potential, while a stereotype might be said to occupy the space squarely produced by possibility alone. Expectations put limits on what can be while acknowledging that such limits are not fixed in place" (45). Song's point is a hopeful one: there are expectations that constrain Asian Americans, but these expectations, whether of the model minority, the math and computer genius, or the karate kid, do not define us.

In *Racial Feelings: Asian America in a Capitalist Culture of Emotion*, Jeffrey Santa Ana makes a compelling argument linking capitalism, affect, and race: "capitalist economics has created an enduring culture of feeling that affects racialized perception. . . . A capitalist culture of emotion influences the way Americans have understood themselves on the basis of their desires, drives, and interests. It also affects how they've identified other people different from themselves, particularly those who come from another country, speak a foreign language, have a different skin color and physiognomy, and thus appear racially dissimilar. . . . The racialization of Asian Americans has been and continues to be specific to economics" (4–5). For Santa Ana, it is not simply stereotypes or expectations but a "structure of feeling," a set of emotions and affect, that is generally involved in the formation of Asian Americans as a race group (22). For example, Asian Americans' "affects of remembering, . . . their negative emotions, are contradictions to the comfort of belonging in America, instigated by the attempt to live up to the ideals of liberal personhood and individualism" (22). Thus, though they often experience fear and anxiety, as well as happiness and optimism, Asian Americans still hold the American dream central to their mode of cultural expression.

With her emphasis on self-discipline, self-sacrifice, and acquiescence to a Confucian belief in parental authority, Yale law professor Amy Chua has recently resurrected the link between the American dream and the myth of Asians as model minorities in her *Battle Hymn of the Tiger Mother*. Chua's allegedly tongue-in-cheek memoir about bringing up her daughters with high expectations of academic and musical achievements, and depriving them of children's social activities like sleepovers, has not only pushed her book to the best-seller list but engendered thousands of comments and blogs on parenting. Chua appeared on NPR's *All Things Considered* and on NBC's *Nightly News* and *Today* show (Kolbert), among others. Many have called her theories racist, and some have linked the fascination with Chua's parenting methods and her daughters' success to the fear of China's ascent in global economic power and the outflow of jobs to Asia. As Elizabeth Kolbert notes, "It's hard to believe that Chua's book would be causing quite as much stir without the geopolitical subtext." But many people have taken her parenting manual personally, becoming indignant, angry, critical, or sympathetic.

For Susan Koshy, "The current fascination with the model minority family is also linked to dramatic changes in the structure of the American family over the last few decades and to the seeming imperviousness of Asian American family forms to these destabilizing economic and social effects. . . . Asian Americans have not only become exemplary neoliberal subjects defined by flexibility, high human capital, and opportunistic mobility, but the Asian American family has also come to be identified as an intimate form ideally equipped to reproduce human capital" (346). Chua's Tiger Mother reflects "two mainstays of neoliberal discourse—the values of economic productivity and entrepreneurship" (346). Koshy argues, "In contrast to earlier ideologies of the private sphere as a harbor from the commercial values of the marketplace, in this revised model, the family is restructured around the intensive production and reproduction of human capital. What has gone unremarked in the volumes of commentary on Chua's books is that its appeal lies in her reconception of the family as a solution to the crisis in education, the engine of a knowledge economy. . . . Chua's vision of the family offers a voluntarist, private solution to the problem. Unpaid affective labor, idealized as tiger maternal love, provides a means of subsidizing and privatizing the growth and reproduction of human capital" (347, 348).

In addition to Koshy's astute remarks about the "private solution" to the crisis in education, there are a number of other difficulties about Chua's theories. *Huffington Post* blogger Khanh Ho highlights the fact that Chua does not consider "the uneven starting point that immigrants face when they decide to come to the United States" or that "we are now importing a huge number of workers in the technology sector from India, people who form an intellectual elite and who come from the very best of the best schools." Ho notes, "Chua has turned a blind eye to this glaring fact. She has cherry-picked her examples of success, focusing instead on cultural values, not recognizing that many of these people arrive with distinct advantages." If one looks historically at Asians in North America, those early sojourners who immigrated to California in the late nineteenth and early twentieth centuries, mainly coming from the Pearl River Delta in Guangdong (Kwangtung) and Fujian (Fukien) in southern China, did not all rise to become lawyers and professionals because they were mainly from the laboring classes and were not well educated. In *Saving Face: The Emotional Costs of the Asian Immigrant Family Myth*, sociologist Angie Y. Chung observes that the successful Asian immigrant story comes at a great emotional cost for second-generation children of Korean and Chinese immigrants. These children cope with conflict, abuse, and shame in different ways, sometimes from outside the family circle.

Another glaring problem, as Chua herself acknowledges, is that Chua and her Yale Law School professor husband Jed Rubenfeld define success exclusively as attaining capital and material goods, being accepted at top-tier schools, winning Nobel prizes, and getting on Forbes lists, with little regard for making a difference in the spheres of arts, culture, or politics or fighting for social justice, the environment, or peace. In an interview after the publication of *The Triple Package*, Chua admits, "We're looking at groups that are successful in this very narrow way and we're not saying that this is a happier life or a better life. . . . We are pretty repeatedly clear about how that can be very confining, almost like a prison" (Offman). Yet the response from the media and the general public suggests that this "prison" of economic and professional success is very attractive, raising the bar of the "American dream."

In the last decade, a number of literary and filmic works produced by 1.5- and second-generation Asian Americans and Canadians have queried the means to and the type of happiness by chronicling the unhappy or failed life. Instead of following their immigrant parents' pursuit of the "American" dream through self-sacrifice and hard work, the protagonists of these works feel disenchanted with their daily lives. Many are depressed, and some are haunted by memories of their childhood, including experiences of war, trauma, or refugee camps. Instead of aiming for professional success and economic capital, they look for other ways of achieving satisfaction, emphasizing affective bonds and personal and cultural success. Their disavowal of the work ethic and values of their parents signals a rejection of the narrowly defined road to success that Chua measures, and consequently a rejection, in many cases, of neoliberal capitalism.

Studies on the mental health of Asian Americans and Asian Canadians show that feelings of depression, fears, and instances of failure are present but often not openly discussed. Yanni Rho and Kathy Rho contradict the belief that "rates for anxiety and depression across ethnicities seem to be similar" (151). They found that Asian American children and adolescents experienced high rates of "depression, somatic presentations of distress, anxiety, suicide, substance abuse, and disruptive behavior/delinquency" (151). However, "due to the expected obedience to adults and a lack of wanting to bring disgrace to their families, the likelihood of a somatized presentation of depression, and/or the lack of understanding by the adults in their lives, Asian youth may be more reluctant to share feelings of depression" (151–52). Michael Tayag also argues that "from a psychosocial perspective, all Asian American students are affected by the 'model minority' stereotype—that is, regardless of whether a student is high-achieving or low-achieving, mental health risks like depression and anxiety and social problems occur much more frequently in Asian American youth than youth in other ethnic groups" (27). According to the American Psychological Association, while suicide rates for Asian Americans are not necessarily higher than for people from other racial backgrounds, Asian American college students were more likely than white American students to have had suicidal thoughts and to attempt suicide. In a study examining the effects of poverty on mental health, Morton Beiser and colleagues compared foreign-born children, Canadian-born children of immigrant parents, and children of nonimmigrant parents. They found that although foreign-born children were more than twice as likely to live in poor families, "they had lower levels of emotional and behavioral problems" (Beiser et al. 220). The link between poverty and mental health was "indirect and primarily mediated by single-parent status, ineffective parenting, parental depression, and family dysfunction" (220). That is, economic status does not directly affect children's mental health. Other factors come into play, such as dynamics within the family, emotional distresses caused by dislocation, and trauma from war, refugee camps, and adjustment to a new culture and environment.

The First Decade of the Twenty-First Century: Context for Narratives of Failure

In *Cruel Optimism*, Lauren Berlant argues that "the current recession congeals decades of class bifurcation, downward mobility, and environmental, political, and social brittleness that have increased progressively since the Reagan era. The intensification of these processes, which reshapes conventions of racial, gendered, sexual, economic, and nation-based subordination, has also increased the probability that structural contingency will create manifest crisis situations in ordinary existence for more kinds of people" (11). A number of specific factors and events have negatively affected the conditions of life and work in the last fifteen years, roughly the production period of the works I examine. Robert Perrucci and Earl Wysong point out that in the United States, from the 1970s the early twenty-first century there was "an increase in the proportion of families with upper levels of income and a decrease in the families with middle-level income." Upper-level incomes (over $100,000) grew from 4 percent of families in 1969 to more than 18 percent in 2000 (12). At the same time, middle-level incomes ($25,000 to $50,000) declined from 41 percent to 27.5 percent of families. About one-quarter of all families over this time period had "incomes below $25,000, putting many Americans in the category of 'working poor'" (12). These figures are more worrisome when one takes into account inflation—that is, the difference in the economic power of $100,000 or $25,000 over thirty years. It might look like more people are getting marginally richer, but one-quarter of Americans are getting increasingly poorer. Perrucci and Wysong note that "three out of four families in the United States have very little economic power. Even so-called middle-class families ... find themselves in a constant struggle to make ends meet" (18–19). Taking into account people's "access to essential life-sustaining resources and the stability of those resources over time," Perrucci and Wysong argue that in effect, what we have is a polarized "two-class structure," where the privileged class, "composed of those who have stable and secure resources that they can expect will be available to them over time," make up 20 percent of the population (30–31), and the "new working class, composed of those who have unstable and insecure resources over time," make up 80 percent of the population (31). Though the upper segment of the "new working class" are "comfortable," they are "vulnerable to major economic downturns or unforeseen crises (e.g., health problems)" and have "limited investment capital to buffer such crises" (31).

Similarly, law professor Mechele Dickerson points out that the "American dream," a term first coined by James Trulow Adams eighty-five years ago, may already be dead for some. She notes three characteristics of today's economy: unaffordable housing and a decline in home-ownership rates; downward economic mobility, where "workers are now more likely to be underemployed, ... hold more than one job at a time and quilt a patchwork of paychecks together just to make ends meet"; and retirement insecurity and instability, where "older baby boomers who either have retired or are approaching retirement often find that they have inadequate savings" and "younger Americans are ... struggling to save for retirement" (Dickerson). She concludes, "Americans who have worked hard and played by the rules now fear that they will never be financially successful. They have lost faith in the American Dream. They are disillusioned, and they are showing signs of despair."

In addition, the first decade of so of the twenty-first century is bookended by two world financial roller coasters. At one end is the dot-com bubble of 1997 to 2000: a rapid rise of the stock market in the Internet sector, such as Nortel Networks and NASDAQ, followed by the collapse of the bubble around 1999–2001. At the other end is the failure of U.S. financial institutions in September 2008, leading to a global bank and monetary crisis for the next couple of years. In the intervening years, we witnessed the September 11, 2001, attack on the World Trade Center, an event that changed the perception of American power and hegemony, as many scholars have pointed out. Jean Baudrillard notes, "the whole play of history and power is disrupted by this event" (4), "eighteen suicide attackers, who, thanks to the absolute weapon of death, enhanced by technological efficiency, unleashed a global catastrophic process" (8).

Edward Murphy and colleagues echo other scholars with their suggestion that "the September 11, 2001 terrorist attacks on the U.S. made a significant impact on the American psyche, possibly changing value structures, because this was the first major attack on U.S. soil and more Americans were killed in this attack than at Pearl Harbor on December 7, 1941." Post-9/11 polls showed that people's reactions ranged from "anger, shock, horror, [and] devastation" to sleeplessness and nightmares (Murphy et al. 400). In particular, Murphy et al. focused on 9/11's impact on teenagers and found significant changes to their "terminal values," those values Milton Rokeach explained as the most important goals each person sought in their lives (Murphy et al. 403). Having surveyed one thousand high school students from northern California before and then repeating the survey after the September 11 attack, they found that the top five terminal values before 9/11 were self-respect, family security, true friendship, freedom, and health (414). These values all contribute to one's self-esteem, "sense of accomplishment, inner harmony, pleasure, self-respect, and wisdom" (399). After the September 11 attacks, for these students, as for their adult counterparts, "safety and security values moved up in the hierarchy of importance to replace previously important self-actualization and esteem values" (416). The top five terminal values after the attacks, in order of importance, became "freedom, world peace, family security, self-respect, true friendship" (414). A world at peace, which is described as a world free from war and attack, moved up in importance from sixteenth to second, while many self-esteem and self-actualization values—such as having a comfortable life, a sense of accomplishment, inner harmony, mature love, pleasure, self-respect, and wisdom—decreased in importance (412). This survey reveals that we now have a generation of youths who have internalized the political and media discourse of terrorism and have become more concerned with "safety" and "security" than with their own personal goals and sense of well-being.

For Asian North Americans, particularly South Asian Americans and Canadians, 9/11 and Bush's subsequent discourse of the "War on Terror" spawned a new kind of hypersensitivity to race and religion. In the first decade of the twenty-first century, Middle Eastern and Muslim individuals, and those South Asians who looked Middle Eastern, became the target of racial fear and hatred, replacing blacks (Jim Crow laws from 1876 to 1965), Chinese people (Chinese Exclusion Acts of 1882–1943), and Japanese people (World War II and the economic ascendancy of the 1980s). Similar to the way Nisei (second-generation Japanese Americans and Canadians) were identified as the enemy during the Second World War, and to the way Chinese American Vincent Chin was misrecognized as Japanese in Detroit in June 1982, people from the Middle East, Sikhs, Muslims, and other South Asian Americans and Canadians were lumped together in an undifferentiated category of Other and became identified as dangerous and criminal "terrorists." Indian-born Canadian writer and Giller Prize winner Rohinton Mistry canceled a U.S. book tour in November 2002 after experiencing racial profiling at U.S. airports. He explained that he was "stopped repeatedly and rudely" at each airport along the way—to the point where the humiliation to him and his wife had become "unbearable" ("Racial Profiling"). The term *flying while brown* was used in numerous newspaper and magazine articles to narrate instances of U.S. citizens from Pakistan, Egypt, Iraq, and other countries being escorted off planes or not allowed to board their flights for "security reasons" even though most of these passengers had cleared security (see Polakow-Suransky).

In her insightful article "Transnational America: Race, Gender, and Citizenship after 9/11," Inderpal Grewal points out that "the creation of the Middle Eastern/Muslim as terrorist recuperated in new ways an old category of the Oriental.... Being brown, also known as 'looking Middle-Eastern,' was a racial formation which included South Asians, Arabs, Iranians and many others" (546). After 9/11, this new racial Other was "gendered through its representation of masculine violence, fanaticism and barbarism" (547) through the media and popular discourse: "As the victims of the attack on the twin towers and the heroes who were produced in the aftermath, individuals and families were shown to be heterosexual, firemen were sanctified and the histories of racism within firehouses across the nation were ignored. Photo mugshots of the attackers in the newspapers showed them to be all males, presumably Muslims, represented as fanatical, well-trained, dangerous and thus barbaric" (545). Through global media repeatedly showing images of the attack on the twin towers, many people across the world "felt a horror that they would not have felt for others suffering from violence in other sites and times" (545). Grewal argues that a form of "global grief" was produced: "The spectacle on TV brought together those cosmopolitans who felt in solidarity against the 'barbarisms' of the world with those who watched for news of relatives" (545). Many ethnic Americans, including Asian Americans, made an effort to affirm their allegiances to the United States, assuming hyperpatriotic performances such as displaying, waving, and wearing the American flag.

Compounded with this sense of insecurity about legitimacy and belonging is the fluctuating rate of unemployment for youths aged sixteen to twenty-four in Canada and the United States over the same period. In their review of the effects of the Great Recession on youth labor markets, David Bell and David Blanchflower note that in the United States and the UK, the "young are particularly susceptible to the negative effects of spells of unemployment well after their initial experience of worklessness" (summary). They report that "the performance during the 2000s of the youth labour market in most countries has further deteriorated" from the worsening conditions of the 1980s and 1990s (1). As the table from Bell and Blanchflower shows, in 2010 youth unemployment rates in the United States were at their highest since the 1970s. In Canada they were also high, on a par with the rates of the early 1980s, when the last of the baby boomers graduated from universities and colleges. The reasons for unemployment are varied, ranging from the global outsourcing of manufacturing jobs to China and other countries and the shift in the labor structure toward an increased need for skilled workers (Bell and Blanchflower 11). Unemployment "increases susceptibility to malnutrition, illness, mental stress, and loss of self-esteem, and increases the risk of depression. The unemployed also appear to be at higher risk of committing suicide, and of poor physical health outcomes later in life" (12). Bell and Blanchflower note that youth unemployment is often associated with "increases in burglaries, thefts and drug offences" (12).

Table 1. Unemployment rates for youth aged 16–24

	1970–74	1975–79	1980–84	1985–89	1990–94	1995–99
Canada		13.2%	16.1%	13.3%	15.7%	15.1%
United States	11.6%	13.7%	15.5%	12.2%	12.9%	11.1%

	2000–2004	2005–2007	2008	2009	July 2010	
Canada	13.2%	11.7%	11.6%	15.3%		
United States	11.2%	10.8%	12.8%	17.6%	19.7%	

Source: Excerpted from Bell and Blanchflower.

Not coincidentally, the most popular teen books of the first dozen years of the twenty-first century are those that depict sixteen-year-olds who have to beat the odds, fighting against their peers, governments, or the rulers of their world to survive. Suzanne Collins's *The Hunger Games* (2008), *Catching Fire* (2009), and *Mockingjay* (2010) and Veronica Roth's *Divergent* (2011), *Insurgent* (2012), and *Allegiant* (2013) are all about making the right choices, not knowing which friends to trust, and leaving behind family. They explore anxieties about growing up, but in intensely disquieting, life-threatening surroundings. The most popular genre of the decade is dystopia, compared to the magic, witches, and fantasy of the best-selling *Harry Potter* books of the 1990s.

Some of the most popular TV shows on Netflix are similarly those that are about survival and struggle outside of traditional communities. *Dexter* features a serial killer who hunts down suspected murderers on his own rather than with the Miami Police Department. In *Breaking Bad*, Walter White is a high school chemistry teacher who resorts to creating and selling drugs to help his family survive his upcoming death. *Orange Is the New Black* takes viewers inside a prison to reveal the inadequacies of institutions in protecting the vulnerable and racially marginalized. These shows are much grittier than the popular shows of the 1990s, which included *Friends*, *Sex in the City*, and *Seinfeld*.

Unhappiness, Depression, Failure

This book looks at instances of failure, unhappiness, and depression in selected works of fiction, life writing, and films produced in the twenty-first century. A number of works depict youth who rebel against parents, who react against the myth of the model minority and reject the American dream. But there are other works, not necessarily from a young person's perspective, that also question the definition of success in terms of professional and economic achievement, as well as ones that deal with the lingering effects of trauma, loss, and family separation. The rebellion of second-generation children against their parents' values is not new—we have well-known examples such as Maxine Hong Kingston's classic *The Woman Warrior*, Evelyn Lau's *Runaway*, Fae Myenne Ng's *Bone*, and Brian Roley's *American Son*. Erin Khuê Ninh's *Ingratitude: The Debt-Bound Daughter in Asian American Literature* examines second-generation Asian American daughters' refusal to participate in what she calls the "immigrant nuclear family as a special form of capitalist enterprise" (2). She argues, "Asian American intimate relations reveal themselves to be profoundly ordered by a capitalist logic and ethos, their violence arranged around the production of the disciplined and profitable docile body" (6). In works by Kingston, Lau,

Jade Snow Wong, Catherine Liu, Fae Myenne Ng, and Chitra Divakaruni, daughters are raised under the constant threat of violent disownment should they refuse to enter the "lucrative math- and science-based professional fields now open to them" (Ninh 16–17), or should they exhibit filial disobedience by violating codes of chastity.

There are two crucial differences between the conditions of the 1980s–1990s and those of the first decade of the twenty-first century. One is the marked advances in computer technology and the Internet that gave rise to Web 2.0 and social media. The other is the establishment of ethnic studies, Asian American studies, and local community programs that support cultural and artistic endeavors of Asians in the United States and Canada. First, as Michael Mandiberg notes, the big technological change after the turn of the century was the "access to tools and the invention of new media forms" that allowed "formerly passive media consumers to make and disseminate their own media. New technological frameworks have arisen that center on enabling this media creation: message boards, audience-driven review sites, blogs and comment systems, photo- and video-sharing websites, social networks, and social news sites, bookmark-sharing sites, and microblogging platforms, to name some of the more prominent ones" (1). These new advances are relevant to this project because Asians and Asian Americans are among the biggest users of new media. Betsy Huang notes, "Asian Americans have indeed taken full advantage of new media, making their presence known most substantially on YouTube" (151). Huang cites a number of producers of digital shorts, such as Kevin Wu, Ryan Higa, Christine Gambito, Philip Wang, and others, who "boast millions of views and almost the same number of subscribers" (151), as well as Jennifer Im and Michelle Phan's fashion vlogging. Using new media allows Asian North Americans to circumvent the gatekeepers of traditional mass media outlets like television, radio, newspapers, and film in order to express their views, tell their own stories, criticize or mock aspects of dominant culture, and most importantly, create a sense of the Asian diasporic community. Ryan Wong observes that these artists are important icons for today's culture: "Banal as it might seem, in today's media-dominated America, faces-on-screens are an essential tool of staking a claim in the conversations—cultural and political—that shape this society" (qtd. in Huang 151).

One of the better-known Asian American activist bloggers is Phil Yu, who started *Angry Asian Man* in 2001. Inspired by his Asian American studies classes, the Korean American started the blog after graduating from Northwestern University. He explains that the title "was kind of a joke at first, but it was also chosen to be confrontational and to bust some stereotypes about the quiet and passive Asian" (Choi). The blog, now "a leading voice of the young, savvy, Asian American community" (Choi), publishes comments and articles; shares tweets and links about Asian Americans in politics, culture, the arts, and the news; and makes jokes and critical comments about Asian Americans in the media. It highlights the achievements of Asian American artists and those who do community work on behalf of Asian Americans, and it also calls out racist acts. A practical application of lessons learned from Asian American studies, the blog fosters identity formation, using anger, wit, and humor to articulate resistance against racism directed at Asian Americans.

Second, even though the roots of the Asian American movement can be traced back to the late 1960s and early 1970s and were linked to the energies of the civil rights and Black Power movements (Goellnicht 4), the establishment and expansion of Asian American studies programs across the United States took several years, until as late as the 1990s (Chang 181). Don Goellnicht notes that in Canada, the birth of Asian Canadian literature as a field was even more protracted (1). As a result, Asian North American writers before the 1990s, such as Jade Snow Wong, Maxine Hong Kingston, Joy Kogawa, Amy Tan, and Evelyn Lau, would not have benefited from the kind of solidarity and literary tradition we are now familiar with. They were writing about their experiences, the struggles to assimilate, to reconcile not only with American and Canadian cultural values and society but also with their parents. But to a large extent, they were writing in isolation rather than as a collective. Only in the late 1990s and the early years of the twenty-first century do we begin to see a widespread currency of the counterhegemonic discourses found in Asian American/Canadian or ethnic studies programs.

Going back to the #Asian Fail, #failasian, and #Asianfailure memes, tweets, and Tumblr posts with which I began this introduction, we see that besides requiring social media platforms for their creation and dissemination, they are successful and funny only because there is an audience with a shared knowledge and understanding of the stereotypes, expectations, and issues of diasporic Asians. Asian American content creators, YouTubers, bloggers, and Tumblr makers in the twenty-first century are popular because of several factors: access to computers, Internet, and social media platforms; an audience base or a community of viewers who share a similar historical, cultural, and political background; and ease with their own subjectivities to be able to find distinguishing characteristics that unite the group, allow people to laugh with them, and have enough confidence to confess their shortcomings. In addition, social media sites such as Facebook and Twitter allow for instantaneous connections that transcend national borders. Besides keeping in touch with family and friends, they allow for the "continued, ongoing construction of subjectivity" (Cover 55). Working with Judith Butler's theories of identity performativity, Rob Cover argues that social networking sites help us "process our selves and our actions into coherence, intelligibility, and recognizability" (56). In this case, I would argue that social networking sites enable Asian Americans to perform and reinforce their racialized and critical identities.

Instead of seeing these developments as healthy, some Asian Americans are anxious about them. In her now infamous book about Chinese mothering, Amy Chua reads the rebellious attitude of youth as the "decline" of immigrant generations:

* The immigrant generation (like my parents) is the hardest-working. Many will have started off in the United States almost penniless, but they will work nonstop until they become successful engineers, scientists, doctors, academics, or businesspeople . . .
* The next generation (mine), the first to be born in America, will typically be high-achieving. They will usually play the piano and/or violin. They will attend an Ivy League or Top Ten university. They will tend to be professionals . . .
* The next generation (Sophia and Lulu's) is the one I spend nights lying awake worrying about. Because of the hard work of their parents and grandparents, this generation will be born into the great comforts of the upper middle class. Even as children they will own many hardcover books (an almost criminal luxury from the point of view of immigrant parents). They will have wealthy friends who get paid for B-pluses. They may or may not attend private schools, but in either case they will expect expensive, brand-name clothes. Finally and most problematically, they will feel that they have individual rights guaranteed by the U.S. Constitution and therefore be much more likely to disobey their parents and ignore career advice. In short, all factors point to this generation being headed straight for decline. (*Battle Hymn* 22)

Chua's prediction, like much of the rest of her book, is exaggerated, and her attitude is confrontational. Since the sensational publication and reception of the book, she has tried to tone down her assertions, stating that the book was written "in a moment of crisis" and that it "poured out" like "family therapy" (Chua web page). We know that not all first- and second-generation Asian immigrants "work nonstop" to become professionals, and not all those born in North America will grow up to be spoiled brats. However, there is an interesting correlation between Chua's vision of a generation of entitled children and the kind of attitude shown in works produced by Asian Canadians and Asian Americans in the last ten or fifteen years that I would like to explore.

Several recent works deal with the troubled psyches of Asian North Americans. They are different in tone and subject matter from the stories of first-generation immigrants from the 1970s to the early 1990s, which tended to focus on immigration, assimilation, and the struggle for upward mobility and the "American" dream. Today, an increasing number of narratives delineate the opposite turn: disenchantment, depression, aimlessness, rebellion against the stereotypes of the model minority, and often the negative consequences of the famed hard-working ethos of immigrants. This pattern may partly result from intergenerational conflicts and the "filial angst" erin Khuê Ninh has described in *Ingratitude* (3). Ninh examines the familial pressures that are used to produce the "diligent, docile immigrants' daughter" (2), including techniques such as "debt bondage, discursive disownment, designated failure" (12). But it is also caused by larger social and economic shifts and expectations of the last decade.

Attention to the socio-biographical history of immigrant families like Amy Chua's, for example, provides some explanations about postwar Asian immigrants' overinvestment in professional and material status. Chua's grandparents, originally from Fujian, China, immigrated to the Philippines in the late 1930s to avoid famine, poverty, and political persecution. As Chinese Filipinos (*Lan-nang* in Hokkien or *tsinoy* in Tagalog), they would have been regarded as outsiders or foreigners and not well integrated culturally, socially, and politically into the native Filipino community. Chinese Filipinos were mainly business owners and entrepreneurs. They tended to be family oriented, reluctant to participate in politics and government; instead, they contributed to civic organizations focused on education, health, social welfare, and charity. They were the target of kidnappings and extortion schemes in the 1970s and 1980s. This sense of being a stranger would continue as Chua's mother immigrated to the United States, experiencing a "doubly-diasporized" situation. In America in the 1960s and 1970s, it was again easier for Asian immigrants to accumulate economic capital rather than social, cultural, or political capital. Coupled with the Confucian ethos of responsibility, self-sacrifice, and hard work, the sense of dislocation often propelled these Asian immigrants to channel their energies into economic and professional spheres.

Sociologist Peter Li notes, "It is tempting to romanticize the social mobility of Chinese-Canadians in recent decades as the product of remote cultural elements that encourage diligence, perseverance, and education. Such an explanation is untenable because it fails to explain why those elements should have remained dormant for most of the history of Chinese in Canada, reviving only in the 1980s and 1990s. Much of the mobility of the Chinese-Canadians has to do with selective immigration and changing employment opportunities in Canada" (9).

While Chua sees this shift in values over three generations as a "decline" in the ethics and spirit of the (Chinese) immigrant, I would like to examine this tendency or attitude through different theoretical and social lenses and argue for a more positive reading. For one thing, as a phenomenon in our culture, the sense of entitlement to own brand-name clothing, running shoes, and the latest electronic gadgets is not specifically a second- or third-generation Asian immigrant attitude. A recent article in the *Globe and Mail* notes that parents in North America are "spoiling our kids rotten" and that kids are "entitled, narcissistic, oversupplied with tech goodies" (Timson). Elizabeth Kolbert of the *New Yorker* goes so far as to write, "with the exception of the imperial offspring of the Ming dynasty and the dauphins of pre-Revolutionary France, contemporary American kids may represent the most indulged young people in the history of the world" (qtd. in Timson). In China, the generation of Little Emperors— chubby, spoiled urban children who grew up eating McDonald's—has given way to a new generation of "Precious Snowflakes" who are "wrapped in cotton wool from day one" and are hypochondriacs who drink nothing but Evian water (Malcolm Moore). These stories may be slightly exaggerated, but my point is that there is a general tendency for the middle-class youths of Generations X and Y to be more self-absorbed and narcissistic because social and economic conditions have allowed it.

In keeping with this trend, a number of Asian North American works produced in the twenty-first century feature protagonists who are anxious, disturbed, and desiring more or different things than what their parents have to offer. They tend not to pursue the American dream through hard work, as their parents would have. Ninh notes, "Read through the family's economic aspirations, or a parent's class and national investments, Asian American intimate relations reveal themselves to be profoundly ordered by a capitalist logic and ethos, their violence arranged around the production of the disciplined and profitable docile body" (6). Some of the protagonists in the works I study in *Asianfail*, such as those in *Red Doors*, *The Debut*, *Saving Face*, *Cover Me*, and *Skim*, face parental pressures to succeed in the professional or corporate world. However, a number of other works, such as *The Gangster We Are All Looking For* and *Certainty*, depict subjects who are suffering from trauma, or from what Marianne Hirsch has called "postmemory, . . . a *structure* of inter-and trans-generational transmission of traumatic knowledge and experience" (106). Others, such as *A Tale for the Time Being*, *Singkil*, and *Out of the Blue*, examine subjects who are living through what Lauren Berlant calls the "emergence of a precarious public sphere, an intimate public of subjects who circulate scenarios for economic and intimate contingency and trade paradigms for how best to live on, considering" (3). Berlant argues that "the fantasies that are fraying include, particularly, upward mobility, job security, political and social equality, and lively durable intimacy" (3). This comprehensive list comments on our economic instability, employment trends, and ability to promise justice and equal rights, as well as on private, affective relationships. In short, this is a world that approaches the dystopias depicted in books for teens.

Berlant's list does not include the precarity caused by the events of 9/11, but Alex Gilvarry's *From the Memoirs of a Non-Enemy Combatant* takes a darkly entertaining look at the pretentiousness of the fashion industry and the consequences of a Filipino being misidentified as a terrorist in New York. The protagonist, Boyet Hernandez, whose memoir is punctuated by quotes from his favorite fashion designers, writes his "confession" from his detention cell in Guantánamo Bay to try to convince the authorities that he is not a terrorist. The humor comes from the juxtaposition of his obsessive concern for his appearance with the rapidly deteriorating, serious conditions of his imprisonment. The novel is about the perils of pursuing the American dream in the context of the post-9/11 climate of suspicion. Humor is also used in Keshni Kashyap and Mari Araki's graphic novel *Tina's Mouth*, a more lighthearted representation of nonbelonging and racial misidentification.

Reading Failure

Historically, the confession of failure has been used in various ways to align or dissociate oneself from communities, movements, or ideologies. A number of scholars reexamining the discourse of failure have rendered the concept more complex, noting that in addition to bad failures, sometimes there are good failures. In the introduction to *False Starts: The Rhetoric of Failure and the Making of American Modernism, 1850–1950*, David M. Ball quotes Herman Melville, who claims that "failure is the true test of greatness" (*False Starts* 7). Ball argues that "the rhetoric of failure" has served as "a master trope of modernist American literary expression" (*False Starts* 7). Elsewhere, he proposes *failure* as a keyword "employed by American Renaissance writers to negotiate the putative divide between 'high' and 'low' literature" (Ball, "Archaelogy" 163). He cites Nathaniel Hawthorne, who writes, "America . . . is now wholly given over to a d——d mob of scribbling women, and I should have no chance of success while the public taste is occupied with their trash—and should be ashamed of myself if I did succeed" ("Archaelogy" 164). Ball observes that Hawthorne distances himself from the popular sentimental literature of the day in order to define modernism: "this transvaluative deployment of the rhetoric of failure—failure considered as the highest form of success—takes place on a number of different registers in modernist writing, including but not limited to an affinity for the impossible intellectual achievement, the esteem accorded commercial failures, and the unrelenting return to figures of collapse, exhaustion, and futility" (164).

In light of Ball's observations about the rhetoric of failure, I suggest that we can read the posts and stories with the #Asianfail and #failasian hashtags as ambivalent articulations of contemporary Asian North American youthful subjectivity—not of a sense of a mortifying failure to belong, but of a vacillation between embarrassment and pride in not conforming to or belonging to anything imagined as "Asian." They reveal a sense of relief in their failure to comply with normative expectations of being Asian, and in so doing, they demonstrate a rejection of the kind of professional success lauded by Amy Chua. In *The Queer Art of Failure*, Judith Halberstam points out that "success in a heteronormative, capitalist society equates too easily to specific forms of reproductive maturity combined with wealth accumulation. But these measures of success have come under serious pressure recently, with the collapse of financial markets on the one hand and the epic rise in divorce rates on the other" (2). She advocates looking again at failure, given that failure, she says, "allows us to escape the punishing norms that discipline behavior. . . . while failure certainly comes accompanied by a host of negative affects, such as disappointment, disillusionment, and despair, it also provides the opportunity to use these negative affects to poke holes in the toxic positivity of contemporary life" (2–3). Halberstam employs "low theory . . . and popular knowledge to explore alternatives and to look for a way out of the usual traps and impasses of binary formulations" (2). She defines her take on "low theory" as "theoretical knowledge that works at many levels at once, as precisely one of these modes of transmission that revels in the detours, twists, and turns through knowing and confusion, and that seeks not to explain but to involve" (15). Halberstam is interested in "alternative ways of life," citing as an example Peter Linebaugh's and Markus Rediker's account of piracy and mutineers in the seventeenth and eighteenth centuries—people who opposed the rise of capitalism and proposed alternatives in terms of "how to live, how to think about time and space, how to inhabit space with others, and how to spend time separate from the logic of work" (Halberstam 18, 19).

Halberstam argues, "The history of alternative political formations is important because it contests social relations as given and allows us to access traditions of political action that, while not necessarily successful in the sense of becoming dominant, do offer models of contestation, rupture, and discontinuity for the political present. These histories also identify potent avenues of failure, failures that we might build upon in order to counter the logics of success that have emerged from the triumphs of global capitalism" (19). Following Halberstam's encouragement, I examine instances of failure, rupture, and discontinuity in novels, films, and graphic narratives produced in the first dozen years of the twenty-first century to look at how these texts contest the "logics of success" in our global capitalist society. One difference between the selected post-2000 Asian American narratives and earlier expressions of rebellion is their refusal to conclude with what David Palumbo-Liu calls the "rhetoric of healing," assimilation, and adjustment (*Asian/American* 411). Palumbo-Liu observed that the best-selling Asian American novels of the late 1980s and early 1990s, such as those by Gish Jen, David Wong Louie, Gus Lee, and Amy Tan, "reproduce the conventions of healing" (410), whereby the young, usually second-generation protagonist becomes a "healthy individual, cured of the residual effects of history and politics, ready to meet the modern world" (413). What is left out, Palumbo-Liu notes, are the "ideological questions and contradictions of the social space" (413). Because of the 1980s belief that "the personal is political," one ethnic individual's triumph and successful overcoming of obstacles are seen as a kind of collective deliverance.

The following chapters discuss fictional, filmic, autobiographical, and graphic narratives featuring protagonists who struggle to cope with the demands of everyday life, with work, with bullying, with expectations generated by parents and peers, and with the pain and memories of past trauma. In these narratives, failure manifests itself in different ways: in depression, in suicidal thoughts or attempts to commit suicide, in a disinterest in the Protestant work ethic, in bodily mutilation. These affective responses to the national, familial, economic, and professional pressures reveal the still-intertwined relationship between the capitalist ethos, where the individual is seen as having a duty to prosper and be happy; traditional Confucian values of filial obedience; and the politics of race, ethnicity, gender, and globalization. While all young adults are affected by some of the post-2000 conditions outlined earlier, the added difficulty of being regarded as an alien or perpetual stranger contributes to the stress of many of the Asian North American protagonists in these narratives. Interestingly, there are a number of common threads in these works, suggesting that the precarious conditions have not just affected the young, but have a far deeper influence across generations. Parents of the protagonists are having problems with their marriages or have divorced (*Singkil, Saving Face, Skim*);

fathers attempt suicide or become violent (*Tale for the Time Being, Red Doors, Gangster*); grandmothers are overburdened by secrets of the past (*Obaachan's Garden, Lola*).

At the same time, the precarious conditions have generated a cluster of marvelous books and films that use a wide range of narrative techniques, including postmodern self-consciousness, irony, humor, elliptic and poetic prose, and multiple story lines. The genres include graphic fiction, graphic biography, memoir, play, puppet performance, postmodern novel, and film. Though different in style, these works question what Susan Koshy, in her discussion of *Unaccustomed Earth*, calls "normative scripts of ethnic and diasporic identity" (362). In addition, plot discontinuities and "temporal ruptures (dropping out, depression) frustrate the linear path of a narrative propelled by model minority aspirations to acculturation and accumulation" (363). The works depict many kinds of Asianfails and breakdowns; however, in chronicling these situations of precarity, the authors engage with and expose the limits of our neoliberal notions of the good life and happiness, and interrogate the duties required by global citizenship.

CHAPTER 1

Precarity and the Pursuit of Unhappiness

Though different in style and genre, Ruth Ozeki's *A Tale for the Time Being* (2013), Mariko Tamaki's novella *Cover Me* (2000), and her graphic novel *Skim* (2008, illustrated by Jillian Tamaki) all feature Japanese North American teens who struggle with identity issues, family instability, self-esteem, and depression. The protagonists are all unable to follow the kind of hard-working immigrant ethos extolled by Amy Chua in *Battle Hymn of the Tiger Mom*; instead, they pursue what looks like a path to unhappiness. The works illustrate the kinds of challenges faced by young Asian North Americans, including bullying, exclusion from peer groups, problems with body image, and concerns about sexuality. While these issues are not new or exclusive to Asian North Americans, recent Asian North American novels and films frequently represent precarity of various sorts—economic downturn, mental breakdown, marriage breakup, and the like—as part of daily life. The tension that results from these situations affect and mark the young protagonists' bodies in disturbingly physical ways.

Contingency and Connectedness in *A Tale for the Time Being*

The defining event in Ruth Ozeki's novel *A Tale for the Time Being* is the tsunami that struck Japan on March 11, 2011 (also known as 3/11), causing extensive damage, claiming nearly sixteen thousand lives, and injuring six thousand others.

Though the tsunami is not presented in great detail in the novel, which is set in Canada and Japan, it is the means by which two very different women become connected—Ruth, a middle-aged Asian American writer who lives on an island in British Columbia, and Nao, a teenager from Tokyo.

Like her first novel, *My Year of Meats*, *A Tale for the Time Being* juxtaposes the lives of two female characters to reveal the richness and interconnectedness of our "universe of many worlds" (Ozeki, *Time Being* 400). Weaving together the "tales" of Ruth and Nao through a postmodern "metafictional" narrative (Hutcheon, *Narcissistic* 1), Ozeki attempts to grapple with a number of pressing issues in contemporary society: global warming and environmental pollution; bullying of youths; the consequences of the dot-com bubble; aging, memory, and Alzheimer's disease; porn and sex work; and conceptions of time and historiography. Nao's diary, which Ruth finds on a beach in Canada, provides the intradiegetic text, or narrative within a narrative, that brings to life Tokyo's Akihabara district, cosplay, manga, and other Japanese subcultures for North American readers. Ruth's and Nao's narratives reverse the traditional divide of Old vs. New World by locating Asia, rather than America, as the hub of excitement and a place to be discovered.

My reading of *Time Being* explores the ways in which Ozeki plays with the connectedness of geographical space as well as how she illustrates global economic and social uncertainty, or "precarity" and "cruel optimism," in today's society (Berlant 192, 24). Berlant defines "cruel optimism" as "a relation of attachment to compromised conditions of possibility whose realization is discovered either to be *im*possible, sheer fantasy, or *too* possible, and toxic. . . . Cruel optimism is the condition of maintaining an attachment to a significantly problematic object" (24). Berlant argues that there is a "spreading precarity" that "provides the dominant *structure* and *experience* of the present moment, cutting across class and localities" (192). She notes, "What makes the present historical moment a situation is not just that finally the wealthy are experiencing the material and sensual fragilities and unpredictability that have long been distributed to the poor and socially marginal. It is that adaptation to the adaptive imperative is producing a whole new precarious public sphere, defined by debates about how to rework insecurity in the ongoing present, and defined as well by an emergent aesthetic" (195). In *A Tale for the Time Being*, the tsunami, a fascination with death and suicides, and numerous instances of reversals and quick changes in circumstances present a world of precarity that Ozeki tries to offset by presenting us with alternative worlds and time periods, by focusing on characters who seek fulfillment through spirituality and the creativity.

Ozeki's novel and Berlant's study both explore the ways in which people have stayed "attached to conventional good-life fantasies—say, of enduring reciprocity in couples, families, political systems, institutions, markets, and at work—when the evidence of their instability, fragility, and dear cost abounds" (Berlant 2). In *Cruel Optimism* Berlant considers the ways in which "people manage the incoherence of lives that proceed in the face of threats to the good life they imagine" (10). Instead of seeing traumatic events as exceptions to the ordinary, Berlant conceptualizes "crisis ordinariness" or a "notion of systemic crisis" to characterize the lives of people in the United States from the 1990s to the end of the first decade of the twenty-first century (10). Her book looks at "exemplary cases of adjustment to the loss of this fantasy of sustenance through the engaged construction of an archive of the impasse or transitional moment" and considers "what thriving might entail amid a mounting sense of contingency" (11). She observes, "The enduring present that is at once overpresent and enigmatic requires finding one's footing in new manners of being in it. The haunting question is how much of one's creativity and hypervigilant energy the situation will absorb before it destroys its subjects or finds a way to appear as merely a steady hum of livable crisis ordinariness" (196).

Ozeki's *A Tale for the Time Being* is a novel about contingency, about people living "for the time being," as the title suggests, showing how one artist and one teen cope with the "mounting sense of contigency." In the novel, Nao's family, particularly her father and Nao herself, have been through a series of disastrous events, what Berlant would characterize as "crisis ordinariness" (10). Nao's family moved from Japan to Sunnyvale, California, when she was three after her dad was "headhunted" for a great job in Silicon Valley. According to fifteen-year-old Nao: "everything was great and we were just cruising along, except for the fact that we were living in a total dreamland called the Dot-Com Bubble, and when it burst, Dad's company went bankrupt, and he got sacked, and we lost our visas and had to come back to Japan, which totally sucked because not only did Dad not have a job, but he'd also taken a big percentage of his big fat salary in stock options so suddenly we didn't have any savings either and Tokyo's not cheap" (43). For Nao, the move back meant an awkward return to the country where she was born, but where she could no longer function because she "identified as American" and her conversational skills in Japanese were very limited (43). What is significant about the family's change of fortune was its reliance on the "good life fantasy" based on the traditional patriarchal family. Nao notes, "When they went to America, Dad insisted on doing it the American way, where the Man of the House makes all the Big Financial Decisions, but as it turned out, what with the business of the stock options, the manly American way turned into a disaster" (51). When they go back to Japan, the father is unable to find a job and bets on horses instead to try to keep up the illusion of being the family breadwinner. When his wife discovers the truth, he tries unsuccessfully to kill himself by jumping in front of a rapid express train.

Nao narrates these events with an evenhanded, wry, and detached tone that contrasts with the situation's enormous tragedy. She writes, "The Chuo Rapid Express Incident was a major turning point for us, even though we all pretended it never happened. After the incident, Dad started withdrawing from the world and tuning into a *hikikomori* [recluse]" (69–70). Her mom finds a job in a publishing house, but Nao still feels displaced and is unable to stay in the house with her dad, "since he was depressed and suicidal" (73). Nao's mother is afraid that "he might do something crazy like those fathers in America who shoot their children and wives with hunting rifles while they're asleep in their bedrooms then go down to the basement and blow their brains out, except that in Japan because of the strict gun-control laws, they usually do it with tubes and duct tape and charcoal briquettes in the family car" (73). Nao, who has been reading newspaper articles about "suicides and violent deaths and suffering" because she wants to prepare herself for her dad's death (74), becomes addicted to these stories. For Nao, shocking events are no longer extraordinary but have become part of her everyday existence. To show how these problems, of depression, suicide, and loss of job and personal dignity, are not singular occurrences but have become frequent and are happening elsewhere, Ozeki here has Nao refer to crazy "American" fathers who shoot their children and wives. The fantasy of capitalism has failed middle-class workers in the United States and in Japan, and Ozeki's novel depicts people living what Berlant calls "the bad life—that is, a life dedicated to moving toward the good life's normative/utopian zone but actually stuck in what we might call survival time, the time of struggling, drowning, holding onto the ledge, treading water—the time of *not-stopping*" (169).

Nao faces another kind of precarity in her daily life. Not only does she become fascinated by suicide after her father's attempt to end his life, she experiences violence and bullying at school because she is a little older than the other Japanese students and is a recent transfer student. She compares the everyday encounters with her classmates as hunters and prey, as a "pack of wild hyenas moving in to kill a wildebeest or a baby gazelle" (48). She writes, "by the time we got through the doors of the school, I was usually covered with fresh cuts and pinching bruises, and my uniform was all untucked with new little tears in it made by the sharp points of nail scissors, that the girls kept in their pencil cases to trim their split ends. Hyenas don't kill their prey. They cripple them and then eat them alive" (48). With the collusion of a substitute teacher, the students ignore her at school one day, pretending that she is absent while she is sitting in their midst. And for a prank, they hold a funeral for her, film it, put it on the Internet (107), and send her the link. She describes her own (fake) funeral in a deadpan voice: "My funeral was beautiful and very real. All the kids in my class were wearing black armbands, and they had set an altar on my desk with a candle and an incense burner, and my school photograph, enlarged and framed and decorated with black and white ribbons. One by one my enemies took turns going up to my desk and paying their respects to me" (106). In this description, Nao has become estranged from her own body and sees herself from afar. She is even able to appreciate the beauty and solemnity of the joke. Unable to turn to her father, who is depressed, or to talk frankly to her mother, who does not seem to have time for her, she hides the bruises and cuts on her body. She even writes with sympathy about the substitute teacher's cowardly behavior: "I hope you understand that I don't think he was a bad man. I just think he was very insecure and could convince himself of anything, the way insecure people can" (78). She seems to have accepted her classmates' intolerable acts as part of her everyday world while trying to keep up the semblance of the "good life" by pretending that everything is okay with her family. Her epistolary journal, written for anyone who cares to read it, functions as a record of her trials and at the same time is a call for help.

It is this diary that connects the middle-aged writer Ruth in Canada with Nao in Japan. Ruth's discovery of Nao's Hello Kitty lunch box on the beach near her remote island home in British Columbia links the two worlds together. Ruth's reading of the diary makes her into a sympathetic reader/listener, a person who, in feminist philosopher Kelly Oliver's terms, "bears witness" to the oppression of others (18). Oliver argues that "subjectivity develops through address and addressability from and to others" (88). In other words, "only when someone else listens to me can I listen to myself" (88). In Nao's case, her classmates have denied her what Axel Honneth calls "moral recognition" because they deny her her "legal existence" by marking her absent when she is in class, and they have not given her any "social solidarity," the sense of self-esteem that comes from being valued for accomplishments not shared with everyone else (paraphrased by Oliver, 46–47). At one point, Nao likens her writing of the diary to the way "some Christian people talk to God" (*Time Being* 136), appreciating the fact that someone is willing to listen. While Nao has no way of knowing that someone will read her diary with avid interest and share her burdens, Ruth's interest, understanding, and sympathy are conveyed to us, the readers of the novel, and we too become "witnesses" not only of Nao's struggles, despondency, and sense of alienation but also of their effect on Ruth and her husband. Ruth becomes very indignant at times on Nao's behalf, even getting angry at her husband's lame responses to the diary: "The girl is attacked, tied up and almost raped, her video gets put up on some fetish website, her underpants get auctioned off to some pervert, her pathetic father sees all this and instead of doing anything to help her he tries to kill himself in the bathroom, where she has to find him—after all that, the only thing you can say is Babette is cool?" (293). The structure of the novel, with its alternating narrators, co-opts us into becoming empathetic readers like Ruth, who can then give the kind of positive recognition of Nao that others in her world do not.

Another one of Nao's problems is confusion about her sexuality and gender. As she writes in her diary, she wonders whether the imagined reader is a man or a woman. She writes, "It's not such a big deal anyway, male, female. As far as I'm concerned, sometimes I feel more like one, and sometimes I fell more like the other, and mostly I feel somewhere in-between, especially when my hair was first growing back after I'd shaved it" (299). Her feelings of gender uncertainty are not atypical of the experiences of high school students for whom "issues around sexual orientation commonly arise during adolescence" (Williams et al. 47). In their study of sexual minority adolescents and bullying, Trish Williams, Jennifer Connolly, Debra Pepler, and Wendy Craig found that "bisexuality and questioning one's sexuality were more commonly endorsed self-definitions of sexual orientation than were gay male or lesbian" (54) and that youths who questioned their sexual orientation "reported more hostile peer contexts than did their heterosexual peers" (55). Nao recounts "dates" she had for a month with a "guy who worked for a famous advertising agency" who had "loads of cash and suits and watches" (*Time Being* 299). At sixteen and still a virgin, she lets him take her to a Love Hotel in Shibuya, and weeps when they can't have intercourse. Only when she takes off her wig and puts on his shirt, silk necktie, and pants do they successfully make love. The relationship is mostly sexual, with both of them enjoying cross-dressing, but it comes to an end when her hair starts getting longer. She is heartbroken when he vanishes but finds no sympathy from her friend Babette, who originally set them up. The only person whom she can turn to is her great-grandmother Jiko.

Ozeki employs an overtly postmodern fantastic device to resolve Nao's heartbreak, loneliness, depression, and various predicaments. Toward the end of the novel, Ruth dreams that she swims to a shore and encounters the people she has been reading about in Nao's diary. With the help of Jungle Crow, a kind of trickster figure, Ruth goes to Nao's father and stops him from committing suicide by urging him to help his daughter, who also is in despair and about to kill herself (351). Ruth rouses him from despondency by convincing him that he is loved and needed by his daughter, and he responds by going with his daughter to great-grandmother Jiko's bedside. Jiko leaves them with a one-character poem message, 生, *sei*, meaning "to live" . . . "for now, for the time being" (362). Jiko, a Buddhist priest, is one of the few characters in the novel who helps Nao. She does so by teaching Nao to find inner peace through zazen meditation. Nao refers to it as finding her "*SUPAPAWA*" and says, "Zazen is better than a home. Zazen is a home that you can't ever lose, and I keep doing it because I like that feeling" (183). After Jiko's death, Nao's father says, "We must live, Naoko! We have no choice. We must soldier on!" (369).

As in her first novel, *My Year of Meats*, a number of scenes are echoed, linking the worlds of Nao and Ruth and revealing the similarities in their lives in spite of the differences in their age and location. For example, in the chapter following Jiko's death, Ruth visits the cemetery where her own mother was buried. She remembers her mother's death as a "low-key affair" (370) but wonders whether Nao became a victim of the tsunami, as nearly sixteen thousand people died or vanished. Both women are shown in the act of remembering and honoring an older female relative who influenced them.

North America is linked to Asia through the fragile ocean that lies between the countries. The discovery of Nao's diary on the beach presents Ozeki with the opportunity to write about global environmental issues. Ruth's husband, Oliver, theorizes that the lunch box containing Nao's diary could have been carried from Japan to the British Columbia coast through one of the great planetary gyres, perhaps the "Turtle Gyre," so named because the "sea turtles ride it when they migrate from Japan to Baja" (13). He also explains that within these gyres are garbage patches containing plastics and other kinds of waste that do not decompose but are "sucked up and becalmed, slowly eddying around. The plastic ground into particles for the fish and zooplankton to eat" (36). These patches are large—"the Great Eastern Patch is the size of Texas" (36)—and as environmentalist Charles Moore writes, these plastics are a "brand-new kind of despoilment" because they are not biodegradable. Instead they "photodegrade, a process whereby sunlight breaks them into progressively smaller pieces, all of which are still plastic polymers" and accumulate "as a kind of swirling sewer in the North Pacific subtropical gyre." The gyres in the Pacific Ocean are a physical manifestation of the transnational and global connections that are developing between Ruth and Nao and between the United States, Canada, and Japan. Environmental degradation and the despoilment of our oceans and natural world add to the sense of precarity in both Ruth's and Nao's lives.

Ozeki also makes political and geographical parallels between North America and Japan. At one point, Ruth remarks on thematic ties between the colonial history of the island on which she lives and the Miyagi coastline where Nao lives, which was hit by the earthquake and tsunami in 2011. Ruth notes, "Miyagi prefecture ... was one of the last pieces of tribal land to be taken from the indigenous Emishi, descendents of the Jomon people, who had lived there from prehistoric times until they were defeated by the Japanese Imperial Army in the eighth century" (140). Ruth and her husband lived on Cortes Island, "named for a famous Spanish conquistador, who overthrew the Aztec empire" (141). The island's nickname, the "Island of the Dead," may be a reference to the "bloody intertribal wars, or the smallpox epidemic of 1862 that killed off most of the indigenous Coast Salish population" (142). One link between the two areas is a history of displacing indigenous people for ways of life that are not necessarily progressive but exist for the time being.

Media also links the women, and the 9/11 attack in New York reveals the vulnerability and connectedness of our world. Along with the rest of the world, Nao and her father in Tokyo and Ruth in North America watch the planes crash into the twin towers on September 11. Nao's father becomes fascinated with falling bodies: "For the next couple of weeks, he hunted for [people who jumped] on the internet" (267), finding a morbid fascination with the images on screen. Ruth and her husband Oliver were caught in Wisconsin at the time of the attacks and had to drive to the Canadian border to make their way back home to British Columbia. As critics have noted, 9/11 became one of the most "witnessed events in tele-visual history" (Howie 4), and media enabled us to make it into a grand spectacle: to "witness, capture, record, and replay over and over again 9/11, other acts of terror and their consequences" (Howie 10). For Nao and her dad, the Falling Man of 9/11 becomes a figure with whom they identify. Nao speculates about what her dad might be saying to the man on the screen, "What made you decide to do it? ... Do you feel alive or dead? Do you feel free now?" (*Time Being* 268). Imagining what it would be like to be trapped inside one of the buildings, Nao thinks that she and her dad would just have found their "way to an open window.... counted to three ... and jumped" (268). Her wry acceptance of the horrific events of 9/11 reveal the extent to which she is existing at a crisis point; violence and death have become acceptable and banal. For Ruth, the events of September 11 make her see the stark difference between the aggressively macho and patriotic attitude of Americans, who were encouraged by the president to "hunt down the terrorists ... dead or alive" (271), and that of her neighbors on her island in Canada, where "news of the world had little relevance to their daily lives" (272). She remarked on their relative insularity: "from their fog-enshrouded outpost on the mossy margin of the world, she watched the United States invade Afghanistan and then turn its sights on Iraq" (272–73). Unlike Nao's morbid fascination with the falling man, Ruth's age, the location of her home, and her stable life give her distance from the events of 9/11.

Ultimately, the novel suggests that our imagination and our ability to love others are what make us good human beings who can overcome the limitations of space and time. Through her great-grandmother Jiko, Nao gets to read the letters of her great-uncle Haruki (Jiko's son), who was studying philosophy and French at the university when he was drafted into the army during the Second World War. This subplot not only takes us to another geographical location but moves us back in time to 1945. In military school, Haruki was beaten and bullied because he was an intellectual and a peaceful boy. Though he was trained to be a suicide bomber, he could not become the "warrior" that the military wanted him to be. Nao becomes fascinated with him and compares herself to him, seeing the triviality of her life in comparison with his heroism: "Haruki #1 was only a couple of years old than you, but he was a superhero, and brave and mature and intelligent. He cared about his education and he studied diligently. He knew about philosophy and politics and literature, and he could read books in English and French and German as well as Japanese . . . You, Yasutani Naoko, are pitiful compared to him. What do you know about? Manga. Anime. Sunnyvale, California. Jubei-chan and her Lovely Eyepatch. How can you be so stupid and trivial!" (261). Nao comes to understand that Haruki did not want to die and wished only that he could stop time so he didn't have to. His ghost visits Nao during Obon, the time when spirits "would come back from the land of the dead to visit us here" (209). Honored by the visit of this brave and intelligent man, she gradually becomes less self-absorbed and more interested in the life and histories of the people around her.

The novel ends with Ruth reaching out to Nao by writing her a letter and acknowledging her existence. Though she realizes how foolish it is to care about a woman who may or may not still be alive in a country across the Pacific Ocean, she says, "I care whether she's dead or alive in this world" (400), affirming the power and effect that Nao's writing and storytelling have had on her. In Ruth's and the reader's mind, Nao, like the experiment of Schrodinger's cat (see *Time Being* appendix E), exists in a paradoxical state of being both "dead and alive, at the same time" (414). Instead of offering us a "real"-time solution to Nao's depression, Ruth presents Nao (and us) with an invitation appropriate to a novel questioning the boundaries of space and time: "I also just want to say that if you ever change your mind and decide you would like to be found, I'll be waiting. Because I really would like to meet you sometime. You're my kind of time being, too" (403).

Embodying Pain in *Cover Me*

Unlike Ozeki's *A Tale for the Time Being*, Mariko Tamaki's first novella is a short, more local and personal account of teen rebellion, depression, and slow recovery. Tamaki's *Cover Me* and her graphic novel, *Skim*, illustrated by her cousin Jillian Tamaki, depict the perils and troubles of teen girls by using innovative genres that appeal to a younger generation of readers. These texts do more than narrate the story of a rebel adolescent in high school; they suggest the yearning for and possibility of a different world that is beyond what Marxist critics call the production and reproduction of labor. The protagonists of these works of the twenty-first century do not want to be part of the world that their parents have created. Using affect theories by Judith Halberstam and Sara Ahmed, I read these texts in a way that does not categorically see these youths as disappointments in the way Amy Chua implies.

Cover Me, set in 1996 in Toronto, is a fictional account of a young Japanese Canadian woman, Traci Yamoto, who is "out of sorts with herself, her family, and seemingly the rest of the world" (Chen). The ostensible story line is told from the first-person point of view, a narrative about a twenty-year old who has arranged to meet her business executive father for lunch at 12:15 sharp. On the way to and during lunch at the Pink Pearl Restaurant, the narrator makes wry observations about the city and about the people around her. Through flashbacks triggered by various objects and through word associations, she provides vignettes of her childhood, including her mother's nervous breakdown, her own predilection for self-mutilation, and her own suicide attempt. However, similar to Nao's voice, the tone is detached, filled with irony and humor, allowing for a critical reading of contemporary North American/Canadian society.

Traci's father's main concerns in life are ownership and money, and he views his relationship with his family through economics. At nine, when Traci fights with her dad about her "privacy" and "her stuff" in her room, her dad simply says, "This stuff is mine. I paid for it" (Tamaki 15), walking out with her sweater. In contrast to this attitude, Traci is sensitive, artistic, and anxious. Describing her father's job, she says, "For the past twenty-five years my father has worked in one of those skyscrapers in the concrete forest of the Toronto business district. Penis country, my friend calls it, because of the plethora of phallic symbols and suits. King Street, a Mecca of concrete contrasted by a few, small, ill-looking, token trees in little grey corporate cubicles. It's a land without pity, sucking the life out through the souls of my shoes as I puff thoughtfully on my cigarette and survey the secretaries in their business suits and Nikes, basking like seals in the sun. Modern seals, with protein drinks and outrageous Visa bills" (11).

This description connects the business world with sterility, hypermasculinity, and mindless animals. Corporate secretaries are "basking like seals" in their name-brand clothing, mindlessly following trends. Though she respects her father, she feels alienated from his world of business. On the way to lunch, Traci gives some money to a woman begging for spare change because she likes the sign the woman is holding up, which says, "*goin' crazy, wanna come?*" (34). Her father disapproves of her munificence.

Measuring success through professional and economic achievements, like Amy Chua, the father sees his daughter as a failure. However, in her book *The Queer Art of Failure*, Judith Halberstam reads failure and stupidity differently, "as a refusal of mastery, a critique of the intuitive connections within capitalism between success and profit, and as a counterhegemonic discourse of losing. *Stupidity* could refer not simply to a lack of knowledge but to the limits of certain forms of knowing and certain ways of inhabiting the structures of knowing" (11–12). Halberstam points out that "success in a heteronormative, capitalist society equates too easily to specific forms of reproductive maturity combined with wealth accumulation" (2). This kind of belief in acquisition and mastery is something that Traci cannot live with.

In contrast to her father's certainty and solidity, for much of her young life, Traci has felt unsure and jittery. She notes, "by the time I was eleven, my house was one big boobytrap. . . . I was hyper-aware that the clumsiness of my fingers, the loudness of my voice all too often set off a reaction in my mother. I could be upstairs brushing my hair and *snap*, an explosion downstairs" (Tamaki 35). Her inability to cope with her parents and her inability to socialize at school cause her to withdraw into herself. While teen stories of rebellion against parents are not uncommon in Canadian literature (Munro, Toews) and even Asian Canadian literature (Fong Bates), Traci's rebellion is a battle fought on her body. Her body bears the scars of the family's breakdown and her unhappiness with her father's aspirations. By sixteen, she becomes depressed and begins to cut her legs: "I cut to assure myself I was in control. I cut into my thick skin to relieve the pressure bubbling underneath. I had thick skin. And it was slowly ripping apart" (47). Rachel Lee notes that the "embodied experience of self-cutting . . . taps into a twisting of the interior and exterior," where one uses one's own biomaterials to make a statement (36). In the context of torture, Elaine Scarry points out, "physical pain is able to obliterate psychological pain because it obliterates all psychological content, painful, pleasurable, and neutral" (34). Traci's body becomes a site of the unspeakable tensions in the family, the spectacle and reminder of the unsuccessful visible minority.

One day, she accidentally cuts herself too deep and ends up in the psychiatric ward at Sick Kids Hospital, where she realizes, after a day, that she will never be able to follow in her father's footsteps. Instead, she discovers that she can sing: "I surprised myself by being a rather good singer" (Tamaki 60). Singing makes her feel "whole. . . three dimensional" (61), she tells her doctors. Her "string bean Goth" friend Jeff encourages her to join his band, Cover, and she becomes its lead singer. Instead of continuing to cut herself to express her emotions, she starts to get tattoos: "Unlike feeling my scars, feeling my tattoos gives me a sense of power. I am the mistress of my domain" (107). Thorsten Botz-Bornstein argues that "the current fashion for feminine tattoos has changed the idea of the tattoo itself," destroying "conventional female identities such as 'neatness, diligence, appliance, femininity, passivity" (241). He writes, "The new feminine tattoos transgress merely symbolizing functions as they allow for the emergence of an alternative space in which not only right and wrong, but also purity, desire and the self adopt a new, ambiguous status. . . . The tattoo is no longer an inscription functioning as an intimate label but a message written on a wall that can be interpreted in various fashions. . . . tattoos create a new, dynamic, interactive space" (Botz Bornstein 241–42). Interestingly, Mariko Tamaki's own body is heavily inscribed with body art, which makes it very tempting to see *Cover Me* as partly autobiographical.

FIGURE 3. Mariko Tamaki bookfans photo

Touring and singing with the band, the protagonist of *Cover Me* eventually finds a way to express herself. It is through art—singing, covering her body with tattoos, and being with her group of friends—that this sense of self-fulfillment is achieved rather than through her family or the corporate ladder. In *The Promise of Happiness*, Sara Ahmed writes, "The happy family is both a myth of happiness, of where and how happiness takes place, and a powerful legislative device, a way of distributing time, energy, and resources. The family is also an inheritance. To inherit the family can be to acquire an orientation toward some things and not others as the cause of happiness. . . . we are asked to reproduce what we inherit by being affected in the right way by the right things" (45). Tamaki's book suggests just such a rejection of the "right things," or at least of the values that society considers "right."

Adolescent Desires in *Skim*

In *Skim*, a graphic novel illustrated by her cousin Jillian Tamaki, Mariko Tamaki similarly presents an adolescent girl who is trying to find her social and sexual identity. Kimberly Keiko Cameron, a biracial Asian Canadian high school girl, has difficulty with the kind of immigrant hard work ethic required by a Tiger Mom. The novel, set in the 1990s, features "an overweight grade 10 student stuck in the suburbs at a private girls' school, dealing with her separated parents, absorbed in wicca, tarot cards, astrology, and philosophy, and rebelling against conformity" (Saltman). As reviewer Judith Saltman notes, the "tale is narrated as excerpts from Skim's diary. . . . Each entry begins with 'Dear diary' and portrays the day in text and art, creating an immediacy and intimacy at the centre of the story." Like the protagonist in *Cover Me*, Kim, who is called "Skim," is sensitive and artistic, interested in writing and drawing rather than conforming to the expectations of authority figures such as her parents and teachers. Illustrated in black, white, and gray, the work conveys much emotion through facial expression, bodily gestures, and the extreme close-ups of a number of panels.

A number of verbal and visual techniques are used to convey Skim's outsider status, her broken family, and her difficulties in being accepted by her peers. Verbally, the graphic novel tells the story at three levels: the diary that Skim writes is italicized to evoke a hand-written script, the dialogue between characters is set inside balloons, and a first-person interior monologue is printed inside frames. Visually *Skim* does not follow traditional sequential graphic narratives. As Monica Chiu observes, "As if to underscore the confused, alienated, and nontraditional protagonist, no page is drawn in tradition (staid, regular, expected), nine-panel comics format: three panels across, three down, each separated by a gutter. Rather, images are enclosed by variously sized squares, both framed and unframed, the latter sometimes bleeding images (inked to pages' edges)" (Chiu, *Drawing* 31). Through these narrative techniques, Tamaki is able to move the narrative forward and give us background information about Skim's family. For example, early on, Skim tells us that her parents are separated by showing a framed photograph of her father and mother taken in happier days, contrasted with their disparaging opinions of each other written separately underneath it (Tamaki and Tamaki 10). In the narrative's present time, a scene of Skim eating dinner with her mother is illuminated by a lone lamp suspended above, emphasizing their isolation. The stark lighting, the mother's grim expression, and the scant table setting look more like an institution, a prison, than a cozy home. To further emphasize Skim's isolation, the mother is shown in the next panel talking to Skim with her back to Skim (and to us) as she is washing dishes. Within one page, Tamaki and Tamaki depict a happy past and a more forlorn present, at the same time as they comment on the deterioration of the mother-daughter relationship through an upside-down mug drying on the counter that ironically reads, "World's Greatest Mom" (10).

Visually, *Skim* is dynamic and exciting through Jillian Tamaki's unusual framing, the variation in panel sizes, and the use of "dialogue balloons and lines to show movement" (Saltman). At one point, Skim goes to a costume sleepover birthday party as the cowardly lion from *The Wizard of Oz* only to find that all the other girls have dressed up as ballerinas and figure skaters. Sometime during the night, the girls chase Skim and an adoptee from Vietnam named Hien out of the house. There is no need for verbal commentary about racism or exclusion. The two Asian Canadian girls wait outside the door, but they are not called back to the party. The illustration following their expulsion from the party shows Skim alone in the dark from an aerial view, walking home, in a large, one-page, stark black-and-white drawing (Tamaki and Tamaki 87). The perspective dwarfs her and emphasizes her isolation, estrangement, and loneliness. At the same time, the tail hanging from her cowardly lion costume reminds us that she is just an adolescent in a costume and lightens the scene, suggesting that these are the vicissitudes of growing up.

More often than not, Kim is drawn with her head down, signaling that she is unhappy, sulky, or feeling left out. Monica Chiu argues that what is unique about the graphic narrative is the use of the "visual rather than prose" to emphasize anxiety over "sexuality and race" (*Drawing* 27). Chiu notes, "*Skim* exploits the symbiotic affinity between what is visually represented and what is read through verbal silences and across gutters (spaces between frames)" (29). She examines how illustrations, such as the one of Kim and her friend Lisa walking through the woods, show that John (Lisa's gay boyfriend, who committed suicide) haunts them (24–25). Here, I want to extend Chiu's insightful reading about Kim's homosexuality to notions of happiness. Kim is unable to participate in what Sara Ahmed calls the "happiness commandment," which for many girls "means *taking up the cause of parental happiness as her own*" (*Promise* 58). Ahmed writes, "We can think of gendered scripts as 'happiness scripts' providing a set of instructions for what women and men must do in order to be happy, whereby happiness is what follows being natural or good" (59). At one point, Kim recounts her experience of a happiness exercise at school in which students had to write on the board what made them sad and what made them happy. While other students noted that "love," "friends," and "pets" made them happy, Kim had a hard time coming up with an answer, so she wrote, "art." Talking to her best friend, Lisa, she asks incredulously, "Your family makes you happy?" To herself, she thinks, "Lisa is full of crap" (Tamaki and Tamaki 63). Kim is unable to share what she feels with her peers partly because she is attracted to Ms. Archer, her drama and English teacher, who told her that she has "the eyes of a fortune teller" (13). Kim and Ms. Archer's very brief affair is narrated not in words, but in a full two-page illustration set in what appears to be an idyllic forest near the school. The large illustration of the scene of the kiss, without any dialogue, powerfully conveys Kim's ecstasy and, at the same time, the secrecy and unnarratability of their relationship.

Not only is there an overt prohibition of relationships between teacher and student to overcome in her love for Ms. Archer, but Skim, like many gay and lesbian individuals, has to battle societal heterosexism as well as internalized homophobia. Karine Igartua, Kathryn Gill, and Richard Montoro study the links between internalized homophobia and psychological distress, "particularly depressive and anxious symptoms" (25). They examine the "measure of worthlessness or low self-esteem specific to this population," particularly to their "fear of being discovered to be GLB" (Igartua, Gill, and Montoro 25). Jillian Tamaki uses extreme contrasts between light and dark to show Skim's anxiety. Daytime scenes at schools have light, white backgrounds, while Skim's lonely journey to Ms. Archer's house, much like an unattainable knight-errant's quest, is depicted in illustrations that are dark and scary. The often wordless visuals are enough to drive the narrative and to illustrate Skim's nervousness and fear as she goes by herself to Ms. Archer's home to drop off a letter. In a panel that takes up more than half a page, Ms. Archer's home is represented as a Gothic-style house lit from behind by a sliver of moon (Tamaki and Tamaki 50). Jillian Tamaki's close-up of the slot in the door, Skim's legs, and the black background highlight the silence and secrecy of Skim's actions, her adventure. Even the gutters are black, creating the effect of merging the panels, lending a mysterious and clandestine quality to the scene (50). Skim's obsession with and love for her teacher, which she cannot even share with her best friend, demonstrates "how closeted high school culture is" (Saltman) and how delicate and fragile Skim believes her world to be. For Skim, her love for her teacher is at once terrifying and pleasurable, exciting and scary, like a Gothic romance.

However, the lesbian romance is only part, albeit a large part, of *Skim*. The work is closer to a graphic bildungsroman, as the young protagonist experiments with a number of different social scenes and takes on various subject positions, including daughter, rebel student, romantic, artist, and friend. One way of showing her multiple identities is through framing. As illustrated in the lion costume scenes, one of the most distinctive elements of Jillian Tamaki's illustrations in *Skim* is the way she deploys high and low angles, distance and close views to emphasize and pull away from situations. In the beginning of the book, when Skim is very interested in Wicca and is studying to be a witch, her "altar" is depicted in a medium close frame, with items such as her chalice, lavender, tea lights, cloth, and crystals neatly labeled (Tamaki and Tamaki 14). During this phase of her life, Skim and her friend Lisa attend a ritual in the woods one night, where a coven of hippies gathers to call upon spirits. Skim's aversion to the slightly smelly strangers, who use the circle as a kind of AA therapy session, is revealed through close-ups of the people who come forward with their stories, contrasted with her white-colored blank face against a white background after the leader touches her chest. The extreme close-up of Skim's face and the light pencil sketch against a white background stands out starkly on the page, revealing her disappointment and disgust with the so-called spiritual leader and the coven (19).

Another narrative thread in the novel that reflects a bildungsroman's search for identity is Skim's changing friendships. Between the start of the novel, which takes place in the fall, and the end, which takes place at Christmastime, Skim's closest friendship shifts from Lisa Soor, an outsider like Skim, to Katie Matthews, one of the most popular girls in the school. These friendships reflect her changing perspective, her social status in the school, and her self-development. At the beginning, Skim and Lisa's marginal status is shown by a full-page illustration of Katie Matthews surrounded by a bevy of girls at their lockers. The camera angle of the viewer is slightly low, and the bare upper legs of the schoolgirls wearing very short miniskirts are emphasized (11). The angle magnifies their height, and as readers, we, like Skim, look up to them, even as Katie is depicted in sorrow, dumped by her boyfriend, John. Skim and Lisa, though feigning disinterest and feeling superior to Katie and her boyfriend troubles, nevertheless talk about her a lot: Lisa is "not making her a card" (32); Katie "fell off her roof" (45); she is "sooo perfect" (97). They are spectators to Katie's drama, illustrated in one instance by Lisa's separation from Katie's group in the girls' washroom by a dark wall (21) and later by an illustration of Skim and Lisa on one page looking at a group of girls carrying books for Katie, whose broken arms are in casts, featured on the facing page (68–69).

By part 3, Skim and Lisa's world expands somewhat as they develop other interests and form new friendships. Lisa befriends a girl named Anna, while Skim and Katie begin to bond. Lisa and Skim also experiment with double-dating two "car-less" boys (123). The changes to Skim's life are signified by her attempts to change her physical appearance. She bleaches her hair and gets rid of unwanted facial hair, asserting, "mostly I think change is a good thing. Especially when things are crap to start off" (127). She begins to spend time with Katie, and the splash page of Katie and her at Skim's house depicts Skim enjoying herself, throwing her head back and laughing out loud at something Katie is doing (138)—a very different stance from her usual posture, which is with her head down and miserable. Unlike Lisa, who is now in love with a boy, Skim's passage to adulthood is less straightforward. Rejecting her earlier goal of becoming a witch, she continues to explore the woods alone, but has found a number of alternatives and outlets for her creative spirit.

The themes raised in the graphic novel—depression, lesbian love and crushes, cliques of popular girls, and broken homes—are far from the expressed or implied concerns of first-generation immigrants like Amy Chua, with their gauge of success based on economic and professional achievements. While *Skim*, unlike *Cover Me*, does not overtly critique capitalism, it does suggest an aesthetic and an approach to life that are very different from the world of market, commodities, and money, a world that first- and some second-generation immigrants covet and to which they desire to belong. Skim's penchant for writing and drawing suggests an artistic future, and even though her first love, Ms. Archer, leaves the school at the end, Skim goes on with her life and makes other friends at school. Compared to Nao's high school experiences, Skim's problems are less precarious and life-threatening.

Among other things, these three works are tragicomedies, witty and poignant reminders of the pain and conflicts of growing up. But in their depiction of teen protagonists who pursue unhappiness, they reveal the complicated trials facing young people today as they negotiate their gender, academic, and romantic lives. They also question and challenge the values and assumptions of our contemporary society, the ways we often measure success and cast out those we see as nonproductive members or failures, rendering them as Other and strange.

CHAPTER 2

Que(e)rying the American Dream in Films of the Early Twenty-First Century

Historically, representations of Asians in cinema in the United States and Canada can be divided into roughly five stages or forms. Initially, starting in the first half of the twentieth century, there were Hollywood Orientalist depictions of the exotic or menacing Asian. Notable characters from this period include Fu Man Chu, Charlie Chan, Butterfly, and dragon ladies (see Marchetti chaps. 1–2). From the 1960s to the 1980s, as Jun Xing notes, Asian and Asian American filmmakers "presented viable alternatives to Hollywood's stereotypes and made their impacts known" (87) in the form of critical documentary films. Some of these include the works of Loni Ding and Christine Choy, as well as Renee Tajima's *Who Killed Vincent Chin* (1987) and the video documentaries of Richard Fung. In the 1980s and culminating in the 1990s, many Asian American family dramas, such as Wayne Wang's *Eat a Bowl of Tea* (1989, based on a novel by Louis Chu) and *The Joy Luck Club* (1993, based on Amy Tan's novel) and Ang Lee's *The Wedding Banquet* (1993), entertained and generated interest in the "exotic" customs of the East or represented the cultural tensions between first- and second-generation Asian North Americans (e.g., Mina Shum's *Double Happiness* [1994]). Arising out of the desire to present "countervisions" (Hamamoto and Liu) to dominant cinematic representations and show Asian American "identities in motion" (Feng) are a growing number of films produced in the twenty-first century that reveal the variety of genres, concerns, and directorial and production styles that might be classified as "Asian American" or "Asian

Canadian." Just as it is now difficult to define an "independent" film, it is becoming difficult to categorize "Asian American" films. In his introduction to *Contemporary American Independent Film*, Chris Holmlund writes of "independent" film: "for numerous critics, and many audience members, too, the label suggests social engagement and/or aesthetic experimentation—a distinctive visual look, an unusual narrative pattern, a self-reflexive style" (2). However, Holmlund notes that independent filmmakers also produce hundreds of pulp and horror flicks that do not necessarily show "personal vision" or "alternative perspectives" (2). The same can be said of "Asian American" films, which may or may not have the director's "distinctive visual look" or even be about Asian Americans. In addition to well-known films featuring Asian Americans, auteurs such as Ang Lee, Wayne Wang, and Mira Nair have all made successful mainstream films, including *Sense and Sensibility* (Lee, 1995), *The Ice Storm* (Lee, 1997), *Brokeback Mountain* (Lee, 2005), *Smoke* (Auster and Wang, 1995), *Maid in Manhattan* (Wang, 2002), *Vanity Fair* (Nair, 2004), and others, that feature mainly non–Asian American characters. At the same time, films that feature Asian American characters, such as the box office hits *Harold and Kumar Go to White Castle* (2004) and its sequels, with their Korean and Indian American stoner protagonists, and *Gran Torino* (2008), the first mainstream U.S. film to feature Hmong Americans, were not directed or produced by Asian Americans. The first decade of the twenty-first century also saw an influx of Hong Kong–influenced martial arts and *wuxia* action films that feature a prominent Asian or Asian American actor, such as *Romeo Must Die* (2000) starring Jet Li and *Charlie's Angels* (2000, 2003) with Lucy Liu.[1] Countless Asian North Americans work behind the camera, on screen, and in technical production on many other U.S. and Canadian films (Mimura xv). These developments complicate in positive and expansive ways our understanding of Asian North American representations in film.

In this chapter, I look at a selection of post-2000 Asian American films that feature Asian American protagonists. These films focus on stories of adolescents and young people who are 1.5- or second-generation immigrants. In order to look at the ways filmmakers tell their stories about contemporary life, about growing up as Asian Americans, and about their explorations of sexuality, I examine mainly comedies and dramas set in the contemporary United States and Canada rather than fantasies or action films set in historical time periods or in Asia. While the selected comedies and dramas are mainly realist in their

---

1. For a discussion of Asian American and African American identifications in buddy-cop films, see LeiLani Nishime, "I'm Blackanese."

portrayal of settings and situations, they do employ elements of film subgenres, such as black comedy, romantic comedy, melodrama, and musical comedy, to enliven their stories and show characters' growing disenchantment with their parents' version of the American dream. The young people are depicted in these films as developing creative, sometimes quirky strategies to deal with familial, social, and cultural pressures. The 1.5- and second-generation Asian North American immigrants are different from their predecessors, as they have come of age in a period of rapid changes in media, travel, migration, ethnocultural communities, and technology. Sociologists Jennifer Lee and Min Zhou point out, "Asian Americans comprise a significant portion of today's new immigrants, accounting for one-third of all new arrivals since the 1970s. As the twenty-first century unfolds, the children of Asian immigrants—who are often referred to as the 1.5 generation . . . and the second generation (U.S. born of foreign-born parentage)—are coming of age in record numbers" (xi). The immigration situation is similar in Canada. Statistics Canada reports that the visible minority population, which accounted for 16.2 percent of the population in 2006, is growing much faster than the total population, mainly through immigration. The four largest visible minority groups in Canada in 2006 were Chinese, South Asian, black, and Filipino. In 2011, nearly 70 percent of Canada's visible minorities were foreign-born, whereas 20 percent were ethnic Europeans (Statistics Canada, "2011 National Household Survey"). These statistics suggest a more fluid, shifting body of Asian North Americans who have stronger transcultural and transnational ties than their counterparts of thirty years ago.

One difference between the earlier generation of Asian American writers and those whose families immigrated after 1965, when immigration laws in the United States and Canada changed to a point system, is that children of the earlier generation grew up within mainly white communities, in cultural isolation, rather than within their ethnic communities or within multicultural ones. While experiences of growing up vary depending on one's ethnicity, geographical region, and urban, suburban, or rural setting, in general, the children who grew up in the 1990s enjoyed the presence of diasporic communities that did not exist in the 1970s and early 1980s, except in sporadic enclaves such as Chinatown. Cities including Los Angeles, San Francisco, New York, Vancouver, Toronto, and Chicago saw huge changes in their racial makeup and ethnic diversity in the following two decades, and along with these shifts came changes to the cities' social, commercial, and government spaces and services. In addition, advances in technology and communication have eased the connection between this generation of Asian North Americans and their friends and relatives elsewhere. Thus, the experiences of the cohort of second-generation immigrants who grew up in the 1950s and 1960s are very different from those of the 1.5- and second-generation immigrants who were youths in the late 1980s, the 1990s, or the first decade of the twenty-first century.

Youths who grew up in the 1990s and after have an ambiguous attitude about the kind of Protestant work ethic espoused by the generation of immigrants from after 1965. In an article in the *Washington Post* published in September 2014, Aaron Blake cites a poll from the Public Religion Research Institute indicating that 55 percent of Americans say that "the American Dream either never existed in the first place, or that it did exist but doesn't anymore." Not surprisingly, a larger percentage of college-educated white Americans than black Americans still believe that if you work hard, you'll get ahead (Blake). The responses of Asian Americans were not indicated in this poll, but the percentage would depend on the specific groups asked, and the age of the individuals polled.

Having grown up in American society, many of the protagonists of the films I study in this chapter go through a shift in attitude about professional aspirations, love interests, and their Asian American heritage. In these films, Asian diasporic culture and tradition, including the belief in family, hard work, and sacrifice, are seen as part of their parents' heritage. The culture and tradition are sometimes accepted and sometimes mocked and rejected, but often they are rediscovered in the late teens or early adult years.

Filipino American *Debut*

The independent feature film *The Debut* (2000), directed by first-time Filipino American filmmaker Gene Cajayon, was the first Filipino American film to be released theatrically nationwide. Although it received no backing from major studios and was initially self-distributed, it won the Hawaii International Film Festival Audience Award for Best Feature Film in 2000 and was awarded Best Feature Film Honors by the San Diego Asian Film Festival in 2000. It borrows from a number of genres and subgenres—an immigration narrative, an ethnographic docudrama, a gangster film, and a musical—to tell a coming-of-age story. At the occasion of his sister Rose's eighteenth birthday—her debut—the young male protagonist, Ben Mercado (Dante Basco), confronts several scenarios that reveal many of the issues facing second-generation youths. Traditionally, the debut is an important and elaborate celebration for Filipina women—a large party beginning with a blessing, followed by dances and speeches, with formal dresses, flowers or balloons, and food and drinks. In the film, Rose's debut marks a number of beginnings for Ben. Up to that point, Ben has been hanging out with mostly non-Filipino friends, a Caucasian and a Mexican American. One of his estranged Filipino childhood buddies calls him a "sellout," a "white boy," and a "coconut" because he doesn't hang out with the Filipino *barkada* (group of friends). In the opening scenes, Ben shows that he suffers from what Anne Anlin Cheng calls "racial melancholia," where the raced subject feels "self-denigration" and rejection (16, 17). When his non-Filipino friends make an impromptu stop at his house, he is embarrassed by the smells of cooking that emanate from the kitchen. He does not wish his school friends to meet his hospitable family or have dinner with them, in spite of his mother's warm invitation. His mother laments that she has never met his best friends. The friends look at, touch, and make jokes about some of the typical Filipino wood carvings decorated in Ben's home—a large spoon and fork on the wall, a carved statue of a man whose penis springs open when a barrel is lowered. The small details and objects indicate the ways "souvenirs" can elicit different reactions from first- and second-generation immigrants. As Susan Stewart writes of souvenirs, for Ben's parents, "authentic experience becomes both elusive and allusive as it is placed beyond the horizon of present lived experience, . . . the memory of the body is replaced by the memory of the object," which is "saturated with meaning that will never be fully revealed to us" (133). For young Ben, however, the smells of cooking and these souvenirs from the Philippines are signs of his Otherness and difference, and they become objects of shame. We later discover that unlike Rose, he has not learned to speak Tagalog or bothered to learn about Filipino culture.

On the night of his sister's debut, many things begin to change. Through singing, traditional Filipino dance, line dancing, and hip-hop dance, and through a new love interest, he rediscovers his Filipino heritage and learns more about his family, particularly his father. Ben's education becomes a way for filmmaker Cajayon to indulge in autoethnography, the ethnography of one's own culture, to depict the everyday practices of Filipino youths and their families in the San Francisco Bay area. The film documents the lives of diasporic Asians, revealing their "ways of operating" (de Certeau xi). There are scenes where the teens and young adults play basketball in a makeshift court in the parking lot and behind their homes. At the gym where the party takes place, they hold an impromptu and friendly hip-hop dance competition between the young men and women. The party also features a Filipino DJ and record scratcher. There are loving close-up shots of Filipino foods, such as fried *lumpia* (spring rolls), *lechon* (roast suckling pig), *puto* (steamed rice cakes), and *pancit* noodles. The after-dinner entertainment showcases a traditional *singkil* dance with fans and umbrellas, followed by the singing of a Filipino love song by the father, Roland, played by Tirso Cruz III, a famous Filipino actor and singer who was a teen idol in the Philippines in the 1970s.

What is interesting about the social practices of these film's youths is that they borrow from different cultures and ethnicities (Filipino, European American, African American). The youths have the ability to adapt to and hybridize in different situations. Their clothes and bodily gestures demonstrate that they are constantly negotiating between cultures. Partygoers are dressed in Filipino barongs and ternos or Maria Clara dresses during the first part of the celebration, but they change into contemporary Western jeans and T-shirts when they are outside the party room playing basketball, showing off their cars, or cleaning up. In Judith Butler's sense of the performative as a "regularized and constrained repetition of norms" (*Bodies* 95), they consciously and unconsciously "perform" their ethnic and gender roles. With their peers, they act tough, show each other their mufflers and lowered cars, and carry guns, but with their parents, their bodily gestures change. They lower their gaze, they pay respect to their elders by the "mano" salutation (kissing their elders' hands), and when scolded, they cower before their parents. When Ben gets into a fight with Augusto (Darion Basco), the friend from childhood who has become a thug and a romantic rival, Augusto employs a series of colloquial street-gang insults, calling him, among other names, a "bitch" and a "nigger." Their hybridized identities are also suggested symbolically in their dancing: Ben's sisters' friends learn to dance traditional Filipino folk dances, which are controlled and ritualistic. However, later, they also enjoy the freedom of movement offered by rock-and-roll songs and the cha-cha. At one point, several young women challenge a group of young men to a hip-hop dance competition.

In these films, not only do the 1.5- and second-generation Asian North Americans question some of their own and their parents' aspirations, work ethics, and goals in life, but members of the older generation are also depicted as reassessing the consequences of these paths to happiness and fulfillment. Both the young people and their parents challenge the professional and financial ambitions that were hallmarks of the "model minority" ideal of the economically successful Asian American established in the 1960s. As noted earlier, in the 1960s and 1970s, many Chinese and Japanese Americans were praised for their ability to establish themselves through "hard work, family solidarity, discipline, delayed gratification, non-confrontation, and disdain for welfare" (Lee and Zhou 18). Often wealth and professional success became compensations for the lack of acceptance in other arenas, such as politics, the arts, and culture. By the 1990s, however, this paradigm of sacrifice and deferral of happiness for professional success was taking its toll on some Asian American communities, and it did not adequately explain the dilemmas of many immigrants.

As sociologist Diane Wolf notes, "using a transnational framework" for understanding migration and change, scholars such as Linda Basch, Nina Glick Schiller, and Cristina Szanton Blanc go beyond the "dichotomous notion" of acculturation, a process that goes from native culture to receiving culture (Wolf 459). Instead, "a transnational approach acknowledges multiple locations of 'home' which may exist geographically but also ideologically and emotionally" (459). In her study of second-generation Filipino youths in Vallejo, California, in the mid-1990s, Wolf found that these sons and daughters of immigrants felt great pressures from their parents about their academic studies as well as their social and sexual lives. Often, these children had to accept parental decisions about education, including what to major in, rather than studying an "area well suited to their ... interests and talents" (465). Wolf coins the term "emotional transnationalism" to describe the way second-generation Filipino youth are situated "between different generational and locational points of reference— their parents', sometimes also their grandparents', and their own—both the real and the imagined" (459). Thus, the "model minority" myth only partly explains the struggles of the youths and, in some cases, of the parents of Asian American immigrants.

In *The Debut*, several vignettes reveal how second-generation youths experience some of the problems Wolf describes: difficulty in parent-child communications, sense of alienation, fear of failure, contradictory messages (especially about sexuality), and the need to keep "family secrets" (468–69, 471). Augusto, who functions mainly as an antagonist and foil to Ben, is also pulled by the duties of a good Filipino son and a need to be a leader to his peers. He demonstrates his strength to his group of friends by acting super macho—bringing a gun to the party, bullying others, and showing aggressive behavior toward the girls. His hypermasculine actions can partly be seen as a reaction to his father's death and his mother's remarriage to a Caucasian Asiaphile. Augusto's mother, Alice (Fe de los Reyes), behaves rather ludicrously, speaking loudly, dressing in extravagant clothes, and calling attention to herself by dancing with teenagers. Though rebelling against her, Augusto becomes quiet and submissive to her when she yells at him for fighting, revealing his internal emotional struggles. A different set of values is exemplified by another friend, who gives the boys a lecture about racism in America. As the boys are admiring each other's cars after dinner, he tells them that there is a "car conspiracy" that distracts Filipino Americans from more important information. Instead of focusing their energies on changing their mufflers and lowering their cars, they should be aware of how the United States has engaged in war with the Philippines and how the Filipinos and Mexicans fought to unionize labor. He challenges them to think about why "brown" people who are very interested in cars never make it to the Daytona 500. Though the parking lot at a party does not seem like an ideal place for a lecture about Filipino American history and marginalization, the scene demonstrates the competing perspectives and challenges that face Filipino American youths.

The central conflict of *The Debut*, however, is that of filial obedience versus individual desire. Ben desperately wants to turn down medical school, a career path his father wished him to pursue, in order to become an artist. His career is a source of contention between him and his father, who sees Ben's portraits, graphic illustrations, and paintings as a waste of time, or at best a "hobby." Some of the movie's most moving and insightful scenes are those that depict the relationships between Ben, his father, and his grandfather. The film suggests that the choices one makes in life are influenced not only by one's parents but also by the previous generation, even if this earlier generation is located at a geographic distance. This influence is long-lasting and deep and cannot be vanquished simply by leaving one's birthplace. One can leave one's country, but the pain of familial wounds carries on in the adopted country for years. Roland Mercado, Ben's father, acts like a tyrant, unable to see Ben's creativity and talent at drawing. He has decided that Ben is going to be a medical doctor and is pushing Ben to go to UCLA, where he has been awarded a scholarship. The reasons for his tyrannical behavior are partly revealed toward the end of the film, when we see the way Roland's father, Lolo Carlos (Eddie Garcia), treats Roland. The grandfather, who has traveled to attend the debut party, talks to the father with a condescending attitude. He belittles and verbally abuses his son, mocking him for being nothing better than a postman. He tells him that he has failed as a parent, allowing hoodlums to attend the party. At the party, we find out that Roland had to give up his singing and his band in order to support his family in America. When he is being chastised, Roland becomes subdued and does not answer back, showing a very different side. Toward the end of the film, the father grudgingly begins to appreciate Ben's artistic talents and to disassociate the American dream with economic success. Instead of yelling at Ben again when Ben brings up his desire to study art instead of medicine, the father says, "you talk to your mom about this Cal Arts thing." Implicitly, he is allowing Ben to choose rather than dictating what his son should do, and he is thereby breaking the generational cycle of tyranny and verbal abuse.

Similarly, in *Shanghai Kiss* (2007), a romantic comedy written by David Ren, the protagonist, Liam Liu (Ken Leung), has dropped out of Columbia University to pursue a career in acting. As Liam goes to various auditions, the film shows the difficulty Asian American actors have in finding dramatic roles. Hollywood casting producers still believe in casting Asians in stereotypical "Asian" roles, and Liam finds that either he is not "white" and cannot play certain roles, or else he is not "Asian" enough to play others. In Eric Byler's *Charlotte Sometimes* (2002), the main protagonists are also not upwardly mobile professionals—the lead male character, Michael, works as an auto mechanic, while his secret love interest is an aspiring Hollywood actress. In these representations, Asian Americans are no longer shown to be always eager to conform to and "assimilate" into middle-class America, with its "Protestant, heterosexual, hardworking family" values (see Patricia Chu 15). Instead, these Asian Americans are in the process of negotiating their identities anew, emphasizing what Kandice Chuh terms the "internal instability of 'Asian American'" (9) in order to "imagine otherwise."

What is fascinating about the discovery of the customs, the past, and the "old country" of one's parents is that, in contrast to works such as Amy Tan's novels, the "old country" is no longer figured as one of superstition, snake soup, and ancient secrets. In *Shanghai Kiss*, the "old country" of Shanghai is not a landscape full of backward peasants, mystical tales, and exotic foods but rather a thriving metropolis, with superhighways, skyscrapers, and fast-food restaurants. The Asian American protagonist Liam Liu, brought up in the States, moves to China to settle down for a while after he inherits his grandmother's house in Shanghai. East and West are no longer figured as Old World and New World, where the New World offers progress and opportunities lacking to the Old. Liam has burgeoning love interests in both Los Angeles and Shanghai, but the women he is involved with are not figured stereotypically as modern versus traditional. Instead, the barriers for their romance lie elsewhere. With the young woman from LA, the barrier is her age (she is only in high school, while he is twenty-eight); with the Chinese woman, Micki, there are economic and other barriers, such as her macho boyfriend. While Liam eventually discovers that he is not Chinese enough to live in Shanghai permanently, the option remains open. In the film, travel between the United States and China is convenient and a common occurrence. Although not working full-time, Liam manages to make two trips to China within a short time. Migration is no longer just westward to North America but works in both directions. Liam contemplates living in China, and the reasons for staying or returning have to do with work, family, and other affective ties.

The Happiness Duty in *Red Doors*

In Georgia Lee's debut film, *Red Doors* (2005), an Asian American father spends much of his time rewinding and watching old VHS tapes of his daughters performing ballet and ice-skating as children. No longer able to fully take charge of his family as his three daughters, now grown up, seek independence from their Chinese immigrant parents, the father looks at the past with nostalgia and longing. His act of revision and the mother's wish to cling to traditional Asian customs are tinged with melancholy and humor, as we become aware of the many ways in which their daughters are questioning or deviating from the middle-class values and aspirations of the parents. The quirky, funny, and dark *Red Doors* plays with our expectations of the immigrant narrative by asking what happens after the American dream has been fulfilled. What else is there to yearn for when you have a successful career and own a house in the suburbs of New York? If "the promise of happiness" is implicit in becoming a model minority, how does one deal with unhappiness? (Ahmed, *Promise*). Along with a longing for the innocence of childhood, the persistence of sadness and melancholia in *Red Doors* reveals the gap between the performance of citizenship and the feeling of belonging to the nation. I argue that along with the legal and civic duties of a U.S. citizen, such as obeying laws, paying taxes, and voting, is a social duty of pursuing happiness. In her discussion of contemporary British multicultural society, Sara Ahmed writes, "Migrants are increasingly subject to what I am calling the happiness duty, in a way that is continuous with the happiness duty of the natives in the colonial mission. . . . Citizenship now requires a test; we might speculate that this test is a happiness test" (*Promise* 130). However, what constitutes happiness is contestable. Ahmed notes, "The public investment in happiness is an investment in a very particular and narrow model of the good; being happy requires a commitment to find what [Shulamith] Firestone brilliantly describes as a 'narrow difficult-to-find alley' of human experience" (70). Migrants and minorities, such as the Wong family, who are unable to fit into this narrow alley find themselves at a loss, labeled "dysfunctional" and viewed as unintelligible subjects.

Red Doors debunks the myth of the "model minority" by depicting a dysfunctional Chinese family. The director says, "While my Asian heritage intimately informs my work, I have decided not to place the cultural card front and center in this film. Even though the Wong family is Chinese, I believe that their emotional frays and struggles are universal amongst families of any background. By portraying the characters first and foremost as complicated individuals grappling with real life issues, I hope to present a more human face in place of the often stereotyped image of Asian Americans in mainstream western media" (Georgia Lee). *Red Doors*, which won the Best Narrative Feature award at the Tribeca Film Festival (New York category) in 2005, has been compared to *Saving Face* because they both feature Asian American lesbians (Swartz). Josephine Tsui Yueh Lee has cited it in her study *New York City's Chinese Community*, along with Ang Lee's *The Wedding Banquet* and Wayne Wang's *The Joy Luck Club*, as a film that illustrates the "friction between the new and old ways of life of several generations of Chinese Americans" (8). However, I want to examine it here for its humorous but dark critique of the American dream, for its refusal to fulfill what Ahmed calls "the happiness duty" (*Promise* 7), and for its resistance to representing what Sau-ling Wong calls "sugar sisterhood," the comforting stereotypical images of the Orient for white, middle-class women readers ("Sugar Sisterhood"). *Red Doors* features Asian American protagonists, but in genre it is closer to Sam Mendes's *American Beauty* in its cynicism about suburbia. The trailer for *American Beauty* invites audiences to "look closer" at the façade of comfort and apparent placidity that characterizes the suburbs, and to look at the tensions and disjunctions within the lives of the average American family. Similarly, Georgia Lee invites us to look closer at the successful Asian American family and see the costs of ethnic assimilation and compromise. While reviewer Ed Gonzalez may be right that Lee's film simply follows the "clichés" of indie movies "made fashionable in the wake of *American Beauty*," I contend that its importance lies in the fact that relatively few feature-length films focusing on Asian Americans' day-to-day lives make it to national distribution. Issues raised by scholars in the 1990s, such as the importance of representation, visibility, and stereotypes, are thus still pertinent to today's film and media culture.

One image that encapsulates a number of important themes raised in the film is that of the outsider and borders. This theme is comically brought out by the family's poodle, Lucky, who in a number of instances is put outside the front door of the family home. Via a newly installed invisible fence, Lucky is being trained not to leave the front yard. Invisible fences work by having a pet wear an electronic collar that gives a mild electric shock whenever the animal approaches the border. Significantly, the fence cannot be seen by others but is felt by the wearer. The other character who is often shown in the yard is the father, who at one point accidentally steps in Lucky's feces. At the end of the movie, he stands in the garden and peers through the window to watch what his wife and family are doing inside. I suggest that the father and his three daughters are, like Lucky, negotiating borders, invisible but restricting. They have each encountered fences in their lives that have prevented them from "happiness," from going where they would like to go and doing what they desire.

These "invisible" restrictions include gender and ethnocultural expectations, the "happiness duty" of migrants (Ahmed, *Promise* 7), and the ideologies of the successful, well-integrated middle-class American family. The film captures a summer where all of the family members begin to step outside the safe boundaries of their lives.

For the father, Ed Wong (Tzi Ma), his recent retirement has made him reassess the meaning of life. He makes a series of half-hearted suicide attempts that are interrupted by daily life and trivial duties in his domestic circle. At one point, attempting to hang himself in his study, he steps on books by Sigmund Freud, Hannah Arendt, Martin Heidegger, and Immanuel Kant, but he is stopped by his youngest daughter, who comes in nonchalantly and announces, "Lunch, Dad," all the while listening to the music blaring in her headphones. The scene juxtaposes the carefree, happy-go-lucky attitude of the younger generation and the more serious, meditative attitude of the older generation, but exactly what ails the father is not made explicit. The books suggest an existential questioning about the meaning of life. His obsession with old family videos suggests a yearning to preserve the past, a time when he was able to control and watch over his daughters. Along with the loss of control is the loss of Chinese culture and tradition. At the beginning of the film, the two eldest daughters barely finish an elaborate family meal laid out on the lazy Susan by their mother because they have to catch their trains. In their haste, Samantha (Jacqueline Kim) knocks down a small Buddha statue, an ornament that Samantha says can be purchased anywhere in Chinatown. She measures the figurine's worth as its replacement dollar value, rather than its sentimental or religious value. In contrast, by the end of the film the father goes to a Buddhist monastery in order to find solace and comfort—not to a Christian church, even though the family says grace before their meal. These little signs suggest that his unhappiness is caused by his sense of the inevitability of change but also by the knowledge that Asian traditions and culture are disappearing in his family. This theme is not new to immigrant literature, but the father's way of dealing with loss is both novel and darkly comic.

The father's repeated attempts to kill himself suggest that he is mourning for something and that, in Freudian terms, he cannot "let go" (Ahmed, *Promise* 139). Ahmed notes that in Freud's "Mourning and Melancholia," whatever "grief aims for, one thing is not in question: that we are speaking of a loss in history, a loss that is real, or given in or to history, even if what is lost can be uncertain or abstract" (139). It is not coincidental that the father's depression or mourning becomes stronger when he retires, when he is no longer working to achieve the professional respectability and economic security to which most immigrants aspire. But even then, he is not able to fully articulate the cause of his unhappiness. Ahmed argues, "Migrants as would-be citizens are thus increasingly bound by the happiness duty not to speak about racism in the present, not to speak of the unhappiness of colonial histories, or of attachments that cannot be reconciled into the colorful diversity of the multicultural nation. The happiness duty for migrants means telling a certain story about your arrival as good, or the good of your arrival" (158). Thus, when the story is not happy, one becomes silent.

In *Red Doors*, the father and his eldest daughter, Samantha, are forced to reexamine their careers and achievements in life, assessing the fulfillment of their creativity, familial and domestic needs, and professional ambitions. Samantha, a corporate executive engaged to Mark (Jayce Bartok), a young, ambitious professional man, finds herself questioning the direction of her life when her high school sweetheart, a teacher and musician, accidentally reenters the scene. Even as she is supposed to be finalizing her wedding plans with Mark, she is drawn to the singing and strumming of Alex (Rossif Sutherland), who has come to their old high school to give guitar lessons. She becomes aware of the sterility of her relationship with Mark and of her professional career, and what she has sacrificed in the pursuit of economic and business success. It is significant that she weeps while attending a ballet performance. The show reminds her of her own childhood ballet classes and links her to her father, who is watching home videos of the girls at ballet. Like the father, Samantha weeps for the past, but in her case she mourns the artistic possibilities she has had to quench in order to succeed in the business world. Many second-generation Asian Americans forego artistic aspirations in order to satisfy their parents' desires for practical and secure careers in business, medicine, and other professions.[2] In this film, for the first time Samantha resists the linear progression toward professional success, acknowledging that the prescribed path of the American dream might not be for her.

In the commentary version of the film on DVD, Georgia Lee states that the story of Samantha was based on her own life and that initially, like Samantha, she was working her way toward a successful professional career but then decided to drop out. Her short film *Educated* (2001) is a fantasy and meditation about the excessive parental control exercised by Asian parents. The protago-

---

2. The struggle between parental expectations and a second-generation Asian North American's desire for artistic careers is also the subject of Mina Shum's *Double Happiness*, in which the protagonist is an aspiring actress. See my chapter on Shum in Ty, *Politics of the Visible.*

nist, Alice (Kathy Shao-lin Lee), is a high school student who discovers the aborted suicide of her friend Wendy (Jenna Ushkowitz). Attempting to follow Wendy, she comes upon a series of dreamlike scenes where Asian American children have become their parents' pets and are made to perform—play piano, achieve high SAT scores, greet their aunties in Chinese on command. Tightly leashed (literally) by their parents, these children have become pet automatons in a stifling and nightmarish world of familial obligation and scholastic pressure. In *Red Doors*, this restrictive world, rigidly controlled by Asian mothers, has become more humorous and more nuanced. While the mother, May-Li Wong (Freda Foh Shen), presides over Sunday dinners, her attempts to impose her values upon her family are only partly successful. Sam and she tussle over what color Sam's wedding dress should be—red or white—but her persuasive powers are limited. She is depicted sympathetically in other scenes, as a wife and mother who shows love mainly through cooking, food, and the rituals of domesticity. In another scene, third daughter Katie comes upon her mother quietly weeping in the basement as she folds her missing husband's laundry. She is seen not just as a controlling mother, as in *Educated*, but as a woman who is trying to accommodate her life to her family's changing needs and mores.

Though mainly a romantic comedy, *Red Doors* has overtones of suburban Gothic, where surfaces camouflage underlying violence. The father's depression and retreat to the Buddhist monastery reveal his angst about the meaning of his career and life. Samantha's unhappiness and inability to articulate what is wrong with her hypercontrolling fiancé suggest a deeper sense of anxiety about her life's direction. Their scenes of interaction, in their apartment, are mainly shot in cold, blue-gray colors. Sam does not give up her executive position altogether, but she does end her engagement with Mark and takes some time to go in search of her father. Instead of devoting herself fully to her professional career, she also begins to become more involved with her family, bringing her mother to watch her little sister's hip-hop dance performance. The film suggests that Sam will at least reassess her romantic life and career rather than continuing thoughtlessly in the path her parents have desired.

Another way in which *Red Doors* reworks cultural expectations of Asian American identities is through the comic depiction of the teenage rebel. The third sister, Katie (Kathy Shao-Lin Lee), has brightly colored hair and plays brutal and violent pranks with a boy Simon (Sebastian Stan) from school. The two of them express their attraction to each other by exchanging mischievous gifts: they send each other rats, put burning dog poo on the other's front porch, and give each other a variety of embarrassing sex toys. Her Chinese ethnicity is less important to Simon than her quirky, nihilistic personality. At school, Katie, with a host of other American teenagers of various ethnicities, is on a hip-hop dance team, which practices to music by E-Roc and MCI. Like her father, and like Ben from *The Debut*, Katie starts out as a fully assimilated American but later explores her ethnic and cultural roots. At the end of the film, the mother watches with surprise as she discovers Katie practicing a traditional Chinese dance in the backyard, dressed in a traditional Chinese red costume, albeit with her running shoes on.

Among other things, the film celebrates the power of art, as various forms of art lead different members of the family to epiphanic moments, or at least to short moments of happiness. Listening to Alex play his guitar and watching the ballet both push Samantha to reflect on what might have been. Julie gets the courage to enjoy ballroom dancing with her same-sex partner, while Katie discovers that it can be as cool to learn a traditional Chinese dance as it is to learn hip-hop. For the father, the old videos of his daughters dancing and ice-skating push him to seek answers to why he is so dissatisfied with his life. While there is little chance of turning back the clock and fulfilling their yearning for a more innocent past, the family's spending time together watching their old home movies is a start to a less rigid definition of success.

Sexuality and Queering Desires

In addition to questioning expectations of the Chinese family and neoliberal notions of success, *Red Doors* also depicts an untraditional and nonhetero-sexual relationship. *Red Doors* and Alice Wu's *Saving Face* (2004) both feature narratives about young lesbian women who question "what it might mean to undo restrictively normative conceptions of sexual and gendered life" (Butler, *Undoing* 1) within an Asian American patriarchal family. Both films use the genre of romantic comedy, employing irony, juxtaposition of characters, and juxtaposition of scenes to reveal the humor, shortcomings, and quirks within the Asian American community. In *Saving Face* the female protagonist, Wil-hemina Pang, is a brilliant surgeon who is in love with her boss's daughter, the dancer Vivian Shing. Because of Chinese cultural and community traditions and expectations, Wil is afraid to let anyone know about their romantic relationship. The "coming out" story has a comedic subplot featuring Wil's forty-eight-year-old-single mother, played by Joan Chen, who gets pregnant unexpectedly by a younger man. As Celine Parreñas Shimizu notes, "the film offers new visions and subjectivities that redefine good and bad womanhood for Asian/American women" (271). Another movie, *Charlotte Sometimes* (which was nominated for two 2003 Independent Spirit Awards), also explores erotic and mysterious sexuality that is outside of the usual patterns and arrangements. Director Eric Byler represents muted desire, obsession, and sexuality through the use of mood lighting, muted colors, long takes, and silences, creating emotionally charged atmospheres. The most explicit sex scenes in the film do not involve Michael, the main protagonist. Instead, he is the unintentional and brooding voyeur of a woman he finds desirable. Like *Saving Face*, *Charlotte Sometimes* explores Asian American sexuality outside the parameters of the usual heterosexual couple.

To date, sexuality as a subject has been approached cautiously in Asian North American literature and film because of its vexed history within the community. In the early part of the twentieth century, antimiscegenation laws and "restrictive immigration legislation directed specifically against Asians . . . [did] much to distort and even prevent family formation" (Hamamoto 62). Individual desire and sexual pleasure are not a focus in Asian families and are usually displaced by the need to produce (male) heirs, as shown in Sky Lee's novel *Disappearing Moon Café* and Chu's novel and Wang's movie *Eat a Bowl of Tea*. Colonialization, war, and the presence of the U.S. military in Japan, the Philippines, South Korea, South Vietnam, and Thailand have exacerbated phenomena such as Asian mail-order brides, prostitutes, and hostesses. Darrell Hamamoto notes that "Asian Americans have grappled with a psychosexual self-alienation that stems from a racialized sexuality shaped and sometimes deformed by hostile social forces" (63). According to Monica Chiu, Asians' bodies have been associated with dirt, disease, pollution, and pathology (*Filthy* 7–10). Aside from heteronormative romance leading to marriage, other expressions of sexuality are either overdetermined or repressed in representations of Asians in the diaspora. Celine Shimizu notes, "The fear of sexual perversity, pleasure, and badness can choke the voicing of complex experiences of sexuality and curb the beauty emergent from the chronicles of our sexual histories and the survival of sexual subjection" (5). Thus, narratives by independent Asian American filmmakers that explore other ways of expressing love, desire, and passion are important. They serve to expand our notions of kinship in Asian North American communities beyond that of the patriarchal family. In her book examining Asian American women performing hypersexuality on screen and scene, Shimizu argues that "hypersexuality, performed and consumed pleasurably as well as painfully, expresses yearning for better representations and realities for those marginalized by race and gender" (5). Judith Butler notes that "those who live outside the conjugal frame or maintain modes of social organization for sexuality that are neither monogamous nor quasi-marital are more and more considered unreal, and their loves and losses less than 'true' loves and 'true' losses" (*Undoing* 26–27). As Foucault reminds us, who or what is considered real and true is also a question of knowledge and power (Butler, *Undoing* 27). *Saving Face* and *Red Doors* present alternatives to the institution of marriage and to normative gender identity.

In *Red Doors*, middle daughter Julie (Elaine Kao), a fourth-year medical student, discovers that she would rather dance with a woman than with the men in her ballroom dancing class. The unfolding of her relationship with the movie actress Mia Scarlett (Mia Riverton), who comes to the hospital to research a role, is tender and funny, including an apology consisting of a gift of all flavors of Gouda cheese in lieu of flowers, because that was all the corner store had. Ethnic difference is a muted issue, and even Julie's mother does not make queer sexuality an insurmountable issue. She faints when she sees Julie and Mia kissing in the bathroom, but her shock at the lesbian relationship is short-lived, and she tacitly gives Julie her blessing by the end of the movie.

Taken together, these various scenarios suggest that Georgia Lee refuses to follow the usual immigrant story of movement from outsider to insider, from alien to American. Instead, by beginning with the American dream already attained (the house in the suburbs, the professional career, white boyfriends), the film looks at the road not taken, the cost of conformity, and the implications of the model minority success story. It explores the ways one negotiates between a desire for liberty and the pursuit of a kind of happiness that might not be shared by the larger national body. It also explores borders, fences, or limits—of capitalism, of the Protestant work ethic, of heteronormative gender relations, and of the inexorable need for happiness.

These films about and made by 1.5- and second-generation Asian North Americans still deal with issues of assimilation, stereotypes, and cultural belonging (see Ty, *Politics* introduction). However, many independent filmmakers are also willing to go beyond these themes, tackling issues that go against the grain of ethnic tradition, that are against capitalist and individualist notions of success or against conventional gender and sexual practices. The films reveal the evolving and ever-changing desires, aspirations, and needs of Asians in the United States and Canada. In these twenty-first-century films, ethnic affiliations and racial identities are on a continuum rather than a fixed, essential core. What and who is Chinese American or Filipino American is shaped by many factors, including cultural traditions and teachings, globalization, technological advancements, parental expectations, popular culture, and immigration patterns. These films reveal the shifting values, transcultural affiliations, and desires that are now part of the multiplicity of Asian North American identity (see also the introduction to Ty and Goellnicht).

CHAPTER 3

Haunted Memories, Spaces, and Trauma: The Unsuccessful Immigrant

This chapter looks at two novels that portray what might be viewed as unsuccessful immigrant stories of assimilation and integration. Lê thi diem thúy's *The Gangster We Are All Looking For* (2003) and Madeleine Thien's *Certainty* (2006) feature protagonists from war-torn countries in Southeast Asia—Vietnam and Borneo (later Malaysia)—who start new lives in North America but who carry with them painful and traumatic memories that intrude upon their lives and threaten to overwhelm them. These novels are different stylistically: *Gangster*, told from a child's point of view, is restrained, lyrical, and poetic, while *Certainty* uses multiple narrative strands to tell various stories of loss and trauma. Both novels illustrate the precarity of everyday existence by revealing the ways in which war, death, and violence can lie just beneath a veneer of the ordinary and unremarkable. In lê's novel, space and place are used to suggest a refugee family's state of contingency, both geographically and psychically. In Thien's book, memories and dreams are shown to be mediated by various kinds of technology that enable healing and global connections, even as they reawaken pain and reinforce alienation.

California as the Global South in *The Gangster We Are All Looking For*

California is not usually included in studies of the American South; the longitudinal border usually starts east of Texas. Economically, the state is well off: the median household income for California is slightly higher than the national average (U.S. Census Bureau). In terms of electoral geography, it is a blue state, supporting Democrats rather than Republicans (see Kireev). In terms of an "imagined community," California has more in common with New York than with Georgia or Louisiana.

However, for some groups of Asian Americans, particularly recent Hmong, Vietnamese, and Laotian immigrants, the experience of living in California is comparable to living in the Global South. Unlike the "average" Californian, some of these immigrants exist in a state of liminality, alienation, and transience. What Jon Smith and Deborah Cohn write of the Deep South could apply to these immigrants' experience of California: "the Deep South not as a unified or imagined community but as a scene of the cultural conflicts that white imaginings of community seek to forget, as a locus of literally disciplined bodies" (6). In *The Gangster We Are All Looking For*, lê thi diem thúy depicts the lives of a girl and her family, Vietnamese boat people who arrive in San Diego in 1978. Through the use of a child's first-person point of view, direct and spare prose, and a fluid and nonlinear rendition of time, lê rewrites southern California, specifically San Diego, into an underworld, a space of refugees, the un- and underemployed, and displaced peoples. Place is highlighted right in the opening paragraph of the novel. The young narrator, Mai, says,

> Linda Vista, with its rows of yellow houses, is where we eventually washed to shore. Before Linda Vista, we lived in the Green Apartment on Thirtieth and Adams in Normal Heights. Before the Green Apartment, we lived in the Red Apartment on Forty-ninth and Orange, in East San Diego. Before the Red Apartment we weren't a family like we are a family now. We were in separate places, waiting for each other. Ma was standing on a beach in Vietnam while Ba and I were in California with four men who had escaped with us on the same boat. (lê 3)

The repeated change of location is indicative of the disruptive, shifting, and migrant lives of these refugees who are separated by war, who live in run-down buildings and navy housing, who are frequently relocated, constantly evicted, and always moving.

In the novel, place constructs and delimits familial bonds and community. As Katherine McKittrick writes, "Practices of domination, sustained by a unitary vantage point, naturalize both identity and place, repetitively spatializing where nondominant groups 'naturally' belong" (xv). Examining spaces where people settle reveals not only their socioeconomic condition but also their ways of resistance—the means by which they are able to adapt and indigenize these locales. The first part of this chapter, focusing on lê's use of place, location, and

belonging, participates in the rethinking of borders and the socioethnic parameters of the U.S. and Global South. I want to argue that space, both real and
imagined, is indicative of the liminality and dislocation of the Vietnamese refugee family. Place is also where the past and present converge, where fantasy and
reality meet in the mind of the young protagonist. In lê's narrative, the landscape
of southern California is rewritten, denaturalized, and re-presented, "exposing
how axes of difference—race, sex, sexuality, age, gender, ability, class—inform
and reorder transparent space" (McKittrick 29–30).

The first space that is transformed in the child's mind is the ocean that sepa-
rates her from her mother, left in Vietnam. In the unnamed girl's view, the South
China Sea and the Pacific Ocean are compressed; they become metonymically
the beach where her mother is standing. Instead of giving political borders or
physical dimensions, she gives us an impressionistic view of the exodus from
Vietnam undertaken by her father, herself, and six "uncles":

> The six of us had stepped into the South China Sea together. Along with
> other people from our town, we floated across the sea, first in the hold of
> the fishing boat, and then in the hold of a U.S. Navy ship. At the refugee
> camp in Singapore, we slept on beds side by side and when our papers were
> processed and stamped, we packed our few possessions and left the camp
> together. We entered the revolving doors of airports and boarded plane after
> plane. We were lifted high over the Pacific Ocean. Holding on to one another,
> we moved through clouds, ghost vapors, time zones. On the other side, we
> walked through a light rain and climbed into a car together. (lê 4)

In this passage, geographical space is reduced to the child's immediate sensory perceptions: the boat floating at sea, the beds side by side, the revolving
doors, the clouds and the rain. At her young age, national borders matter less
than her immediate domestic circle, those adults who can give her shelter and a
feeling of security. This creative rendition of space is remarkable for its childlike
simplicity but is also a reminder that the enormity of the family's displacement
becomes buried under a false sense of security in the child's psyche. For the
moment, she feels secure, enveloped by the small spaces of the fishing boat,
the U.S. Navy ship, the crowded beds of the refugee camp, the plane, and the
car. However, the trauma of loss and separation returns and affects her and her
family profoundly as she grows up.

For the first few months, the ocean and everything associated with the beach
remind the girl of her mother. Shortly after arrival, she sees a billboard, "a poster
of a man and a woman at the beach, lying on striped towels, sunning themselves
between two tall palm trees. Above the palm trees were large block letters that

looked like they were on fire: SUNNY SAN DIEGO. The man was lying on his stomach, his face buried in his folded arms. The woman was lying on her back, with one leg down and the other leg up, bent at the knee" (6). Instead of suggesting pleasure, recreation, and relaxation, the scene only reminds the girl of her loss. "I looked through the triangle formed by the woman's tanned knee, calf and thigh and saw the calm, sleeping waves of the ocean. My mother was out there somewhere. My father had said so" (6). Lê reworks the sexuality suggested by the woman's tanned legs in the advertisement into a longing for the mother and, by association, for the motherland. The mildly erotic ad for the sun and the sand is respatialized into a confused site of desire for home in the refugee girl's mind. Homeland and the mother become unattainable objects of desire, revealing how an immigrant subject's psychosexual development may not fit the usual Freudian paradigm.[1] In addition, the girl's reaction reveals the dynamics of colonialization, power, and space. Only those with economic and social stability see spaces like the beach as recreational. For others, they can be a source of threat or danger.

For resourceful immigrants in the novel, space is also adaptable and nego-tiable. A swimming pool can temporarily satisfy the longing for the proximity of the ocean, and a patch of ground behind one's apartment can become a farm. At the red apartment, which they move into after they are reunited with the girl's mother, there is a swimming pool in the courtyard. Although her mother forbids her from using the pool, she appreciates its presence. She says, "it was nice to open the door and have some water" (51). The boys in the neighbor-hood use the pool to escape the drudgery of the poor neighborhood, "diving off the second-floor railing into the swimming pool in the courtyard below" (43). Their risky sport is stopped by the apartment managers, who empty the pool and cover it with cement and rocks. The incident again reveals the link between power and space: the struggle of those lacking authority is frequently illustrated by who can control how space is used. Institutionalized authority governs the "proper" and improper use of space, ensuring that ethnic subjects "know their place."

Water in the novel is particularly fraught. As the novel reveals toward the end, the narrator's brother drowned while jumping between boats in Vietnam. So while water is what links the narrator to her mother when she first arrives in San Diego, it is also a reminder of the past and the family tragedy she has left behind. In addition, lê notes in her epigraph to the novel that "[i]n Vietnamese

---

1. In "Three Essays on the Theory of Sexuality," Freud describes how a healthy child trans-fers his sexual impulses from his parents to other figures (299 & ff).

the word for *water* and the word for *a nation, a country,* and *a homeland* are one and the same: *nu'ó'c.*" One of the women who saw the brother drown said, "He plunged straight down . . . into a hole in the water" (146). For the narrator and her family, water, which is also linked to the nation and country they left behind, is the place of danger and fierce beauty, evoking uncontrollable and passionate affective responses from them even years after they leave their homeland.

Other spaces are similarly governed by forces beyond the family's control. A nourishing and useful garden created by the immigrant community, however marvelous, is short-lived. According to the narrator, there are secret gardens behind the "old Navy Housing bungalows built in the 1940s" (88):

> It is hot and dusty where we live. Some people think it's dirty but they don't know much about us. They haven't seen our gardens full of lemongrass, mint, cilantro, and basil. Driving by with their windows rolled up, they've only seen the pigeons pecking at day-old rice and the skinny cats and dogs sitting in the skinny shade of skinny trees. Have they seen the berries that we pick, that turn our lips and fingertips red? How about the small staircase Ba built from our bedroom window to the back yard so I would have a shortcut to the clothesline? How about the Great Wall of China that snakes like a river from the top of the steep hill off Crandall Drive to the slightly curving bottom? Who has seen this? (90)

This passage reveals how the immigrant community has modified and indigenized local spaces to suit their own needs. A little patch of urban space has been transformed into fertile land in which to grow herbs that are used in Vietnamese cuisine. Significantly, this productive space is invisible to the dominant culture, who see only the "skinny" and poor side of the fence. They are not aware of the luscious red berries and the wonderful "Great Wall of China," which later turns out to be "just a long strip of cardboard" (98). The child's representation of this space challenges, however temporarily, the narrative of marginalization and testifies to the ways in which alternative geographies can be mapped onto familiar spaces.

What is most striking about space in the novel, however, is how locations keep changing. Home for the girl is never stable, but a constant displacement that mirrors the instability and precariousness of the family's existence in the United States. Belinda Kong, who explores the novel's ghosts and doubles, notes that "a geographically anchored site of the home" is "repeatedly denied lê's narrator . . . temporary formations of home are either ironized, retracted or demolished, from her expulsion from the Russells' house, her first foster home in America, which is shown to be as insubstantial and fragile as her hosts' glass menagerie or their very surname that echoes the 'rustling' sound of the butterfly in the paperweight, . . . to her family's eviction from the converted Navy bungalows, which are torn down to make way for more upscale 'condominiums, town houses, family homes'" (132). Lê evokes the narrator's young age and the confusion of space in her mind by using a child's language to describe the different apartments they have inhabited since landing in San Diego. The girl talks about her homes in terms of primary colors: the "green apartment," the "red apartment," and the "yellow houses" on Linda Vista (3). The juxtaposition of the situation's seriousness—the family's constant upheaval—and the primary-school descriptions creates irony and pathos. The girl describes their various homes as another child would talk about colored blocks or shapes. Even the fertile garden is eventually taken away from the family. They receive an eviction notice that obliges them to leave quickly, and only later do they realize that in doing so they would be locked out of their homes and lose access to their possessions. They cannot afford the new condominiums and town houses that are going to replace the old Navy housing. The girl's mother cries about the home and garden they have to leave behind: "I want to know . . . who is doing this to us? . . . I want to know, why—why there is always a fence. Why there's always someone on the outside wanting someone . . . something on the inside and between them . . . this . . . sharp fence. Why are we always leaving like this?" (97).

The mother's questions bring up larger issues about place and power. In California, fences are erected to keep undesirable migrants from entering desirable fertile spaces. For this refugee family, San Diego is not any better than the U.S. South, which, according to Smith and Cohn, "comes to occupy a space unique within modernity: a space simultaneously (or alternately) center and margin, victor and defeated, empire and colony, essentialist and hybrid, northern and southern (both in the global sense)" (9). The liminal spaces that refugees are permitted to occupy are the postcolonial spaces within the First World, suggesting the intersections of beliefs about race, politics, and economics on urban geography. Lê's fictional narrative is an important supplement to our understanding of geographical spaces occupied by Asian Americans in San Diego and in California. Until recently, much of the literature and many of the films about Asian Americans in California have focused on Chinese and Japanese lives and have often been set in Chinatowns or in large urban cities such as San Francisco, Los Angeles, or New York. Vietnamese immigrants' struggles to find their place in other locales have less often been represented.

At the time of the 2000 census, San Diego had "the largest proportion of Asians (15 percent), followed by Los Angeles and New York with 11 percent each" (Barnes and Bennett 7). According to that census, "about 40 percent of the U.S. Vietnamese population resided in California, with most clustering in southern California. San Diego ranked as the sixth most popular metropolitan destination for Vietnamese resettlement in the United States, and the fourth most popular in California" (Espiritu and Tran 373). One important way in which members of the Vietnamese community differ from other Asian Americans is that many of them came initially as boat people with very little: Yen Le Espiritu and Thom Tran note, "even though Vietnamese refugees have made much progress since their resettlement in this country, the poverty rate among Vietnamese in 1990 still stood at 25 percent, significantly higher than the national average of 15 percent" (377). According to Espiritu and Tran, "The 1990 census data for San Diego reveal that the local Vietnamese population appeared to be less well-off than the general Vietnamese population: a higher proportion registered lower education attainments and relied on public assistance" (377). Stories of war in their homeland, of abrupt departure, of refugee camps, of the passage across the Pacific ocean, and of their landing and subsequent acculturation differ from the usual immigration narrative of Asian Americans. Their relation to place and to belonging, both to their homeland and to their host community, is often more fraught and complicated by their refugee exodus and the lack of proper social services once they arrive in America.

In *The Gangster We Are All Looking For*, the young narrator's experience of place is made more difficult by the traumatic memories of her past, a past that involves not only the loss of a homeland but also the death of a family member she feels they have left behind. The memory of her brother's accidental death is buried deep in the narrator's consciousness, signified structurally in the novel by its late appearance. No other family member dares to speak of this lost child. At one point, one of the narrator's friends tells her that she looks like "a boy" and then asks, "Is it true that you had a —" (lê 71). The question is cut off by the girl, who says, "No" (71) in response. However, the brother disrupts her everyday life, appearing as a ghostly presence beside her in the streets of San Diego. A feeling overcomes the narrator as she walks home from the corner store: "Like heat or hunger or dizziness or loneliness or longing. My brother, making no sounds and casting no shadow, was walking behind me. There, again, was the familiar feeling of warmth, of his body beside my body. I could lean back, I could close my eyes and fall down a flight of stairs or off the second-floor railing, and he would be there to catch me; I was certain of it. I need only turn around and there would be his face, his hands" (74). Yet when she tries to tell her mother about his presence, her mother only tells her to "stop it" (76).

Both the girl and her father manifest signs of what Freud calls "melancholia," which occurs when the subject does not have adequate time to mourn and to free "its libido from the lost object" (589). In "Mourning and Melancholia," Freud notes that "the complex of melancholia behaves like an open wound," and sleeplessness is sometimes a symptom (589). Like mourning, it is "a reaction to the real loss of a loved object" (589), but the "melancholic displays something else besides which is lacking in mourning—an extraordinary diminution in his self-regard, an impoverishment of his ego on a grand scale.... The patient represents his ego to us as worthless, incapable of any achievement and morally despicable; he reproaches himself, vilifies himself and expects to be cast out and punished" (584).

One crucial reason for the father and daughter's despondency and melancholia is the unresolved mourning for the brother/son. Because this incident happened right after the war, the father was not allowed to return from his reeducation camp and help the mother bury the boy. The postwar situation and the villagers' superstitious fear of the "bad water" in the boy's body (lê 130) prevented the family from having adequate time and space to mourn. Soon after the boy's body is found, one of the villagers sees the mother's grief but is unsympathetic: "A whole country has to be rebuilt. Does she expect everything to stop simply because she hadn't taken care to keep her own child from wandering too far into the water?" (137). It is not surprising that they are haunted by their memories of his drowning. The father's loss is complicated by the fact that he was away at war when his son died. Although we are not given concrete details about how he spent his time in the South Vietnamese army, we see the effects as the narrator describes her father's restlessness: "Growing up, there were nights when I would hear him staggering in the alley outside my bedroom window. I listened as he tackled the air, wrestled invisible enemies to the ground, punched his own shadow. Drunkenly, he would yell, 'I'm not scared! Come out and fight me. I'm here!'" (100–101). In America, he continues to fight his shadow, or his own memories and nightmares.

In the novel, the girl describes her father as "prone to rages. He smashes televisions, VCRs, chases friends and family down the street, brandishing hammers and knives in broad daylight. Then from night until early morning he sits on the couch in the living room, his body absolutely still, his hands folded on his lap, penitent" (116). The father also suffers from post-traumatic stress disorder from his experiences of war in Vietnam and the subsequent refugee resettlement. In her essay "Vietnamese Masculinities," Yen Le Espiritu explains that "Ba's rage bespeaks the aftermath of gender, race, and global inequality. As subjects of U.S. war and imperialism, Vietnamese masculinity has to be understood within the context of U.S. war in and occupation of Southeast Asia" (91). She writes, "The defeat of South Vietnam battered Vietnamese masculinity, transforming them into fleeing refugees, boat people, and state-sponsored asylees. . . . Vietnamese refugee men in the United States, cast by the media as incapacitated and demoralized objects of rescue, often found themselves at the mercy of white men who had been (re)positioned from defeated foes or allies to valiant rescuers of fleeing Vietnamese" (92). The father claimed to have come "from a semi-aristocratic northern family" (83) and was reputed to be a "Buddhist gangster from the North" in his youth (79). Lê explains that a gangster was an "ideal of someone who could make it work," even if through actions that weren't completely legal (Greenfield Community College). But in America the father loses this power and is unable to adequately provide for and take care of his family.

What the girl fears most is that she will become like her father: "I was certain I saw my future in him. . . . I would disappear into every manner of darkness only to awaken amid a halo of faces encircling my body. Shame would crush me. I would turn away from the people I loved" (lê 116). Sara Ahmed writes of the affective politics of fear: "fear does not simply come from within and then move outwards towards objects and others; . . . rather, fear works to secure the relationship between those bodies; it brings them together and moves them apart through the shudders that are felt on the skin, on the surface that surfaces through the encounter" (*Cultural* 62–63). Father and daughter are very close. When the two first arrive in San Diego, they can't sleep at night. They wander around the "aisles of the Safeway Supermarket" at midnight or "go for walks around the neighborhood and stop to look at the window displays" (lê 110–11). Later, the girl witnesses and is tremendously affected by her parents' fights and arguments. She writes that Ma "is punctuating the pavement with dishes, plates, cups, rice bowls. She sends them out like birds gliding through the sky with nowhere in particular to go. Until they crash. . . . I am in the hallway gulping air. I breathe in the breaking and the bleeding. . . . When Ba plunges his hands into the fish tank, I detect the subtle tint of blood in water. When he throws the fish tank out the front door, yelling, 'Let me see the gangster!' I am drinking up the spilt water and swallowing whole the beautiful tropical fish, their brilliant colors gliding across my tongue, before they can hit the ground, to cover themselves in dirt until only the whites of their eyes remain, blinking in the sun. . . . All the hands are in my throat, cutting themselves on broken dishes, and the fish swim in circles; they can't see for all the blood" (92–93). As Espiritu notes, "lê poignantly depicts the complexity of the father-daughter relationship, one that refuses to be privatized but calls into being the larger history and context of war, refugee resettlement, and chronic poverty" (94).

Other passages suggest that the father feels a compelling sense of loss of place similar to his daughter even after twenty years in California. Images and memories of Vietnam still have a powerful hold on him. Often, he does not answer the phone because he imagines that it will be his father, and that "in just one breath all the heat and the dust of that place; the creaking bicycles; the sound of flip-flops slapping against the road; the old women walking to evening mass; the hawkers at the market; the meager shade in the narrow alleys winding toward his childhood home; the Buddhist monks in their robes, crossing the temple courtyard; the smell of the river; the cemetery filled with red earth and seashells piled high as hills; all this would come coursing through the wires and it would enter his body like a riot of blood" (138). These scenes affect him more forcefully than anything he has experienced in California, suggesting the enormous strength of his affective tie to the homeland he has had to leave. The details in this passage are interesting in comparison to the descriptions of scenes in California. For the refugees, California is stark, unwelcoming, cold. Images of California include run-down apartments, "the abandoned house next door" (55), a "concrete courtyard" (69), a "chain-link fence" (99), and a number of nondescript street names. In contrast, the father's memories of Vietnam are full of people, noises, and other sensory details. In the child's narrative, California appears devoid of color and life, and Vietnam becomes infused with nostalgia and longing. The homeland is a contradictory space of loss and desire, of wonder and yet of peril.

For this reason, the girl feels constricted and trapped within her family and the spaces they inhabit. The first indication of her feeling of entrapment comes symbolically when she tries to free butterflies from a paperweight in the office of the family who sponsored them to California. In her childish mind, the golden brown butterfly "was trapped in a pool of yellow jelly" and she could hear a "soft rustling, like wings brushing against a windowpane" (25). She imagines that it is "the butterfly's way of speaking" (25) and identifies with it and with all the glass animals in the display cabinet. In an effort to free them all, the girl spins around and throws the glass disk, but in the process she breaks the glass case and the collection of glass animals, thereby getting her father and uncles evicted. Much later, as a teenager, she feels the need to flee her dysfunctional home, to get away from her father when he gets into one of his dark moods: "Whereas my father would disappear into himself when haunted, I would leap out of windows and run. If there were no windows, I would kick down doors. The point was to get to the street, at any cost. I would come to see running as inseparable from living. I would choose falling asleep on rooftops and on the lawns of strangers to lying in my own bed, surrounded by knots of memories I had no language with which to unravel" (117). After a while, she does run away from her parents, going to study on the East Coast, as far away as possible by land in America.

However, ultimately, place is also what consoles the family. At the very end of the novel, the father drives the girl and her mother to the beach. There, the girl sees "small silver fish whose bodies gave off a strange light" (158). Earlier, she felt that while her family and the villagers were mourning the death of the brother, he was in fact laughing at them (141). She remembers that "he was stubborn" and would "roll and turn, until like the shells my grandfather had given me, shells my brother had wanted for himself, shells that had been stripped by the sea of all their markings, his body became as smooth and brilliant as polished bone" (146). This passage of transformation recalls the passage in Shakespeare's *The Tempest* where the sprite Ariel consoles Ferdinand by telling him that his father, who drowned in the sea, has been changed into a thing of beauty:

> Full fathom five thy father lies;
> Of his bones are coral made;
> Those are pearls that were his eyes:
> Nothing of him that doth fade
> But doth suffer a sea-change
> Into something rich and strange.
> Sea-nymphs hourly ring his knell. (I:ii, ll. 560–66)

The very last page of the book features the family standing on the beach, looking at the "small, luminous bodies washed to shore" (lê 158). The father turns to the mother and the girl, "smiling broadly" (158), pointing at the fish, as if in recognition and understanding of the transformative and regenerative power of the sea. The water and the beach are the spaces that separated the family, but in the end, the water is also what invigorates and connects them to home and to their loved ones.

Global Desires, Haunted Memories, and Modern Technologies in *Certainty*

Madeleine Thien's first novel, *Certainty* (2006), follows a structure employed by many postmodern novelists—that of telling a story from multiple points of view. This technique has been used by writers to critique what Lyotard calls "grand narratives of legitimation" (qtd. in Fraser and Nicholson 22), to highlight the "politics of representation" (Hutcheon, *Politics* 3), and, in some cases, to emphasize the "presence of the past" (Hutcheon, *Poetics* 4). Linda Hutcheon has argued that postmodernist techniques have been particularly useful for feminist, ethnic, and minority writers who wish to highlight difference: "from the decentered perspective, the 'marginal' and . . . the 'ex-centric' (be it in class, race, gender, sexual orientation, or ethnicity) take on new significance in the light of the implied recognition that our culture is not really the homogeneous monolith (that is middle-class, male, heterosexual, white, western) we might have assumed" (*Poetics* 12). Some well-known examples of Canadian ethnic artists who have employed postmodernist techniques to question the way official history has been written are Michael Ondaatje in his novel *In the Skin of a Lion* (1987) and Atom Egoyan in his film *Ararat* (2002). Ondaatje's novel narrates the experiences of the nameless Macedonian, Polish, and Italian immigrants who helped build the city of Toronto in the early twentieth century, while Egoyan's film represents the suppressed history of the Armenian genocide of 1915 in Turkey. Both works use multiple narrators and multiple time frames to stress the partial and constructed nature of historical representation as well as to emphasize the relevance of the past for people today.

Recently, a number of ethnic writers have resurrected and reconfigured this type of postmodernist fiction for their own purposes. Some of them do not necessarily subscribe to the notion of the loss of master narrative or make use of the playfulness of the postmodern but instead use elements such as decentered and multiple narrators or the presence of the past to demonstrate continuity and connection rather than fragmentation. One recent addition is including the dimension of globality in their representations of contemporary life (see Ty, *Unfastened*, chap.1). By "globality" I mean "a social condition characterized by the existence of global economic, political, cultural, and environmental interconnections and flows that make many of the currently existing borders and boundaries irrelevant" (Steger 7). Manfred Steger notes that globality is different from globalization, which refers to "a set of social processes that are thought to transform our present social condition into one of globality" (8). Novels such as Zadie Smith's *White Teeth*, Salman Rushdie's *The Ground beneath Her Feet*, Ruth Ozeki's *All over Creation*, and Dionne Brand's *What We All Long For* all use multiple story lines, multiple locations, and fragmented narratives to tell the stories of clusters of people who are not necessarily related biologically. More importantly, for the purpose of my discussion, they demonstrate the ways in which human desires and longings and economic and political aspirations cross existing national borders, as well as the ways in which travel, new technology, and patterns of migration influence and construct new affiliations and ways of belonging in our multicultural communities.

These recent works do not simply illustrate the "postmodern conceit that we have no identifiable selves, that we're ever-changing combinations of almost random traits" (Scott) but are concerned particularly with how people and cultures from different parts of the globe connect, mix, or come in contact with each other. The characters, mostly living in diasporic communities, are connected sometimes by chance, by the city in which they live, by the power of the media or pop music, through sharing a cause such as environmental protection, or by a feeling of displacement. Though they no longer live in colonized places, they often carry postcolonial burdens and are haunted by their own personal history. In many of these novels, there is a great deal of movement between countries, even continents. Finally, many of the novels highlight the impact of transnational corporations and changing technology on the physical and psychic lives of displaced peoples.

Thien's *Certainty*, set in multiple locations in North America, Europe, and Asia, is a prime example of one of these global ethnic novels, illustrating connections not only across geographical space but also across time and across cultures. In many ways Thien's novel, although postmodern in form, harks back to the theme of "only connect" (Forster, title page) that was made famous by modernist writers such as E. M. Forster and Woolf. Both Woolf and Forster, for example, believed that although life itself may seem chaotic, one ought to endeavour to look for harmony and wholeness, to try to "connect the prose and the passion" (Forster 188). As Woolf writes, "What is the meaning of life? The great revelation had never come. The great revelation perhaps never did come. Instead there were little daily miracles, illuminations, matches struck unexpectedly in the dark" (*Lighthouse* 150). These modernist writers believed that one should learn to see connections in life that would allow one to act in creative and meaningful ways. Thien's novel uses scenes of loss and mourning to link the lives of a number of characters, in Sandakan, North Borneo; in Vancouver, Canada; and in Ysbrechtum, the Netherlands. The exploration of mourning reveals the ubiquity of grief, as well as the way grief travels and migrates along with the immigrant and the traveler. As in *The Gangster We Are All Looking For*, past grief and haunted memories erupt into the present lives of various characters, constituting a large part of the subject's ethnic or diasporic identity. Ethnic identity, as Michael Fischer notes, is "reinvented" through memory in a way that is not entirely "individualistic," through "revelations of traditions, re-collections of disseminated identities" (197–98). Through ghostly hauntings, repetitive flashbacks, and the return of the repressed, *Certainty* reveals how "the past is not static," how "our memories fold and bend, we change with every step taken into the future" (Thien 110).

In his seminal study of diasporas, William Safran argues that diasporic subjects feel a sense of nostalgia, "collective memory, vision, or myth about their original homeland" (83), but he does not explicitly discuss trauma or bad memories from the homeland. Good and bad memories shape much of the present and future of the diasporic subjects, however. In *Certainty*, through details of "little daily miracles" (Woolf, *Lighthouse* 150) and quotidian acts, Thien shows how contemporary global subjects are produced through a complex "(re)invention" and a "connection to the past" (Fischer 196), a haunted past that is often mediated by machines and digital technology. Memories of the past come in the form of what Bessel van der Kolk and Onno van der Hart call "narrative memory" as well as "traumatic memory" (160). According to van der Kolk and van der Hart, "narrative memory consists of mental constructs, which people use to make sense out of experience" (160), while traumatic memory "occurs automatically in situations which are reminiscent of the original traumatic situation" (163). Unlike ordinary memory, traumatic recall has no "social component" (163), as it is the "painful resurfacing of events of a traumatic nature" (Bal, Crewe, and Spitzer viii). In *Certainty*, Thien narrativizes both kinds of memory, changing those unwanted, inarticulate traumatic visions experienced by her characters, as well as their ordinary memories, into collective cultural memory to be shared with her readers.

It is significant that two of the novel's main characters have occupations that involve dealing with or recording the past. Gail Lim, the protagonist who dies in the opening pages, worked as a radio reporter and radio documentary maker. Sipke Vermeulen, the Dutchman who ends up marrying Ani, the childhood sweetheart of Gail's father, is a photojournalist who later becomes a portrait photographer. Thien's view of visual and audio media is unconventional; it is neither fully modernist nor postmodernist in attitude. For the most part, modernist writers were fascinated with, but also often distrusted, mechanization, machinery, and industrialization. For example, in *Howards End*, Forster associates the business-minded Wilcoxes with "newspapers and motor-cars and gold-clubs," with "telegrams and anger" and lives of "panic and emptiness" (40, 41). Postmodernist writers view with skepticism the excessive use of technology, often criticizing computers, cameras, and other gadgets. A number of Egoyan's early films, such as *Family Viewing*, *Speaking Parts*, and *Exotica*, highlight how our society is surveyed, how those with power use media technology to construct our world for us. Steven Connor writes, "Whereas the modernity refused by modernists was the modernity of urban transformation, mass production, and speed of transport and communications, the modernity refused by postmodernists was that of consumer capitalism, in which the world, forcibly wrenched into new material forms by modernity, was being transformed by being immaterialized, transformed into various kinds of spectacle" (6).

In comparison, Thien depicts visual and audio technology more positively. There is no overt criticism of consumer capitalism or genetic engineering, such as we would find in the works of Larissa Lai or Ruth Ozeki. Instead of conveying an attitude of fear or criticism, Thien depicts machines as necessary and useful apparatuses, almost as extensions of our selves, our bodies, our memories. Writing in the age of MSN, e-mail, and downloadable music and video, many of the writers of the 1990s generation feel comfortable with technology as a part of daily life. Machines help us see and hear things we would miss otherwise. In *Certainty*, Gail Lim is a great fan of audio technology. In her home, "she is surrounded by equipment worthy of a museum. Reel-to-reels, cassette recorders, record players . . . Mini Discs and digital editing programs. . . . She collects tape the way others collect records or rare books, safeguarding them with a feeling of reverence. She has fragments spliced together, dozens of conversations gathered on a single reel. Soundscapes, features, interviews" (Thien 195). When she is twenty-one, a moment of revelation comes when she discovers what a cassette recorder can pick up, catching sounds that humans miss: With her recorder at a marathon, Gail "heard details that she had never heard in life. Whispered conversations, the rhythm of hundreds of shoes striking cobblestone, . . . [her] bicycle bell ringing" (198). She heard "runners drinking as they went, dropping the plastic cups on the road, and the light jaggedness, like cut glass, of their breathing" (198). In another instance, Gail carried "her portable DAT recorder" and "held her microphone out over the water" when three thousand whales were stranded in the "ice-jammed waters of the Chukchi Peninsula" (199). She was amazed to hear "the whales themselves; they formed an endless line as they took turns breathing, one by one, at the air holes" between patches of ice (199). In both these examples, the tape recorders pick up minutiae that unaided human ears cannot. They extend human capability and enable us to see or hear a life beyond the normal level.

Thien's attitude to images is similarly positive. Photographs reveal what our eyes often miss. They can shape our understanding of the past and help us remember. As a young man, Sipke, the photographer, was told that "he had a gift; he was able to catch and distinguish the defining moment. When he was working, he had the sensation of walking into a deep tunnel, the edges of his body dissolving into the scene around him. Yet he was capable—he does not know how or why—of pulling something tangible from the deep" (229). In his work as a war photographer, he has witnessed many brutal scenes, but he cannot help but see some beauty in the pictures:

> In Algeria, he photographed the mutilated bodies of men and women who had been tortured and killed, by guerillas, by the FLN or *colon vigilante* units. He photographed two small children, crawling through the bombed wreckage of their home; and then, that same day, in a neighbouring village,

an entire family who had been murdered, in retaliation, by a mob. He felt as if a part of his mind was decaying, he was ashamed of the pictures that he took, and he was confused by their beauty. A dead child abandoned in a field, his face unmarked, the light on his skin. Tiny flowers rising between his fingers.

Nothing made sense, and he tried to separate himself from his emotions, focusing on the sights of his camera to dull the turmoil, the sickness. (230)

To cope with the disasters and wretched scenes of war, Sipke dissociates himself from what he sees. By viewing the brutality mainly through his camera lens and transforming the traumatic scenes into static art, he is able to distance himself from the nightmares of war.

Thien is not unaware of issues of representation—that pictures and images can produce truth and knowledge. At one point, Sipke remembers another war photographer who wanted people to confront the massacre at Bergen-Belsen. He had arranged and moved the bodies at the site in order to make his photograph more effective. Sipke does not approve of this; he himself tends to view the powers of representation optimistically, relating his photography to truthfulness, a moment of revelation. His attitude toward art is closer to that of the modernists who see art as a means of creating coherence and spirituality amid the chaos of life. He says, "I felt . . . that a photograph could change the way events transpired. The photograph is revealing, it triggers something that you know, a truth that you haven't yet found a way to express. I saw what was happening around me, and I wanted to change it" (238). He recognizes, however, that pictures need some kind of context so that people can make sense of the pieces: "I keep asking myself, what happens when the context is lost and only the image remains? . . . They don't know what happened before or after. All they see is this one moment, disconnected from the past or the future. It feeds their imagination, but it doesn't give them knowledge" (245–46). Instead of being overwhelmed by the violence he photographs, he believes that we can change the world around us: "The picture shows us that this suffering is made by people, and because it is made by us, it is not inevitable. That was the reason I wanted to be a photographer" (246).

In *Certainty*, the issues Sipke raises about images are not tested, and we do not really know if his pictures or Gail's documentaries change people's understanding of events. However, Sipke's assertions work very well as a metaphor for Thien's novel. The novel provides us with several pictures or scenes—some beautiful, some horrible—of a family in Sandakan affected by the Japanese occupation; of Asian immigrants to Vancouver; of a woman from Borneo who moved to the Netherlands to join her Dutch husband. Through the details of everyday life, we are given a portrait, with background and context, of war, migration, displacement, and resettlement. Michel de Certeau has noted that "many everyday practices (talking, reading, moving about, shopping, cooking, etc.) are tactical in character" (xix). They are "ways of operating" that can insinuate themselves "into the other's place" (xix). In *Certainty*, by focusing on and giving voice to seemingly unremarkable characters in remote and not-so-famous places, Thien shifts her readers' attention to these others whose stories are not usually told. Matthew and Ani are both orphans of the colonial war between Japan and Britain; Gail is a journalist and radio documentary maker; and Sipke is a photojournalist from the Netherlands. They lead what can be called "cosmopolitan" lives, in Appiah's sense of the word, where one is "attached to a home of one's own, with its own cultural particularities, but taking pleasure from the presence of other, different places that are home to other, different people" (618). Yet they are not world leaders, bankers, or businessmen in New York, London, or Paris. While Thien does not overtly critique a "master narrative"—of nation, corporation, or institution—her novel has a polyphonic subtlety. Instead of one narrator, one story, there are multiple centers of interest and significance. Matthew, Gail, Ani, and Sipke have interrelated stories that cross continents and oceans. As displaced subjects, they create empowering networks and alliances between them and others they encounter. The new forms of affiliation and community building cross national and even linguistic boundaries—the dinner party hosted by Matthew and Clara Lim, the bonds between Ani and Sipke and between Sipke and Gail.

For dislocated subjects, the need to preserve memories, in the form of a photographic album, an oral narrative, or a written text, is more urgent than for those who remain in their originary culture. Displaced people do not have the immediate family connections or community relations that would allow them to engage in shared cultural remembrance, such as the celebration of events, dates, and other memorials that were important in the places they left behind. Andreas Huyssen observes that in recent years, there "has been the emergence of memory as a key concern in Western societies, a turning toward the past that stands in stark contrast to the privileging of the future so characteristic of earlier decades of twentieth-century modernity" (57). He argues that "memory and musealization [the preservation and categorization of objects in a museum] together are enlisted as bulwarks against obsolescence and disappearance, to counter our deep anxiety about the speed of change and the ever shrinking horizons of time and space" (71). The foyer of Sipke's house is like a museum, with walls full of landscape photographs and pictures of Ani and her child: "the walls are covered with photographs. . . . There are pictures of canals, a field of devastatingly green maize, a windmill that appears to be floating on the water. Among the landscapes are pictures of a woman and a child" (Thien 235). Sipke tells Gail that after Ani died, he "wanted the house to mirror what was in [his] thoughts" (236). Gail feels "a breath of grief move through" her when she sees this memorial (236). Sipke's musealization attempts not only to counter the fast pace and ever-changing landscape of contemporary life but also to find "spatial and temporal anchoring in a world of increasing flux" (Huyssen 74). One consequence of globality is that "the experience of displacement and relocation, migration and diaspora seems no longer the exception but the rule," and the memory of "living in a securely circumscribed place, with a sense of stable boundaries and a place-bound culture with its regular flow of time and a core of permanent relations," seems to be a dream (Huyssen 73, 72). Photographs and sound and video recordings, often transmitted via the Internet or displayed online, now take the place of visits to ancestral homes and homelands, to places of collective worship, or to the cemeteries. The images and technologies replace the absence of collective memories and also function as a way for others to recognize Sipke's loss.

Thien's narrativization of these efforts to remember enable us to understand these Others and to respond to them. The effect of understanding and finding a common ground through grief and mourning is making connection. While postcolonial and ethnic writing of the 1980s emphasized the politics of difference, I see a shift in tendency in the efforts of present-day writers. Thien, like Ondaatje and others, engages in a different kind of politics of recognition, where narrative is used to facilitate a recognition and respect of the Other, not as the same, but not as an object of Othering, either. Political philosopher Charles Taylor, who has written about recognition, explains that the "politics of difference," where "we are asked to recognize . . . the unique identity of this individual or group, their distinctness from everyone else," grows "organically out of the politics of universal dignity" (38, 39). However, Taylor notes that the "politics of equal dignity is based on the idea that all humans are equally worthy of respect" (41) and requires that "we treat people in a difference-blind fashion" (43), an approach that challenges the cultural particularity needed in the "politics of difference." Frequently voiced criticisms of the "politics of difference" include the "reification of group identity," the valorization of "authenticity," and the failure to recognize commonality and form alliances with people from other cultures (McQueen). Instead of espousing the "politics of difference," Thien highlights the fluidity of one's identity, revealing its dependence on location, or what Susan Stanford Friedman has called the "geography of identity" (17). Friedman argues that the new geographics figures "identity as a historically embedded site, a positionality, a location, a standpoint, a terrain, an intersection, a network, a crossroads of multiply situated knowledges" (19) rather than an organic, stable center. Thien's novel demonstrates the ways in which location and geography influence and shape one's identity at a given point in one's life.

Given *Certainty*'s setting in colonial North Borneo, Hong Kong, the Netherlands, and Vancouver, the lines between those who belong to the dominant culture and those who are Othered constantly shift. For example, in Sandakan, Matthew's father, who lived a privileged life under the British colonizers and collaborated with the Japanese army, is ostracized by his own community after the war. The family is doubly displaced, as they are ethnically Chinese but live in Borneo. Later Matthew and Clara immigrate to Canada, joining a multicultural circle of friends there, and he is no longer privileged or ostracized. Sipke, who is Dutch, arrives in Jakarta during a time of strong antiforeign sentiments after Indonesia's war of independence against the Dutch. Signs on the streets say, "Dutch Get Out, Indos Go Home" (Thien 180). Unlike his brothers, who "still live in the village" where they grew up, Sipke is the "restless one, the person who longs to go away, to see the world" (243). He is white and European, but his race does not automatically bring him "race privileges" (Frankenberg 1) when he travels. Thien's characters move fluidly between nations and ethnic communities, looking for happiness, for answers to grief and death. Their lives of movement illustrate what James Clifford calls the increasing mobility of twenty-first-century subjects' "diverse, interconnected histories of travel and displacement" (18).

The characters, scattered all over the globe, share common feelings of loss and trauma. In an interview with Alec Scott, Thien notes that the important thing is not whether one is from the Occident or the Orient: "What binds my characters together, regardless of their background, is that they have so many similar questions." Thien's text, with its multiply-centered narratives, not only provides readers with a glimpse of worlds and histories they have not lived in but also creates for them what Alison Landsberg calls "prosthetic" memories. Landsberg argues that in today's society, films, particularly those about historical events, "enable[] the transmission of memories to people who have no 'natural' or biological claims to them" (18). She notes that "prosthetic memories . . . derive from a person's mass-mediated experience of a traumatic event of the past" and are not socially constructed "in that they do not emerge as the result of living and being raised in particular social frameworks" (19). Rather than see them as false memories, she believes that prosthetic memories have the ability to "produce empathy and social responsibility as well as political alliances that transcend race, class, and gender" (21). While Thien's novel is not a mass visual experience as films are, I would say that her narrative can have the same identificatory effects and create a cultural community based on the affective bonds of grief, loss, and a commonality of experience. Landsberg says, "Prosthetic memory makes possible a grounded, nonessentialist, nonidentity politics based on a recognition of difference and achieved through 'strategic remembering'" (152). Similarly, Mieke Bal and colleagues note that "the memorial presence of the past," or cultural memory, is "the product of collective agency rather than the result of psychic or historical accident" (Bal, Crewe, and Spitzer vii). Almost all of the main characters in *Certainty* "remember" a traumatic event in their lives. Many of these are historically based, though fictional. When he is ten years old, Matthew becomes the unintended witness to his father's brutal killing by Japanese soldiers. Secretly hidden behind trees, he watches while the soldiers beat his father with a rifle, shoot him, and then carry him away in a truck. He is unable to tell even his own mother about what he has seen. Similarly, his playmate Ani, also around ten years old, finds "pieces of clothing, stained," and then discovers her father's body along Mile 8 of one of the Sandakan Death Marches, in which prisoners of war were forced to walk until they died (Thien 44). Her greatest regret is that her father's body had lain "on the airfield for three days" with no one by his side. She worries that his soul will never travel to the place of "food and happiness," as there was no one to guide him (45). Both Matthew and Ani have unresolved issues and intrusive images from their childhood that haunt them later as adults.

For much of his life, Matthew suffers from the trauma of having witnessed his father's murder. Even in Canada, where "the roads are clean and straight," Matthew finds himself still trying "to hold on to his father's voice, the face of his child, the days that marked the end of the war" (47). He has nightmares in which "he tries to tell his father than another path exists, that the centre of his self, the goodness that makes him whole, once lost, can never be recovered" (47). One year after his immigration to Canada, when Matthew, still out of work, becomes a new father, he "began to withdraw into himself, sleeping less or not at all. Day by day, he faltered" (133). His wife, Clara, "could not put her finger on the event that caused this change in him" (133). Readers who have read the flashback narrative, however, understand that his unpredictable moods are symptoms of his unresolved childhood trauma, the kind that Cathy Caruth describes as a "wound of the mind—the breach in the mind's experience of time, self, and the world" (*Unclaimed* 4), a wound that is not easily healed. His daughter, Gail, later remembers him as an insomniac who often became depressed. However, as a little girl, when she asks him about the dreams he has about his childhood, he tells her that his childhood was "like every childhood

...no different" (Thien 206). She remembers that he can give her an account of "how to tap a rubber tree...How to carve an orange into a lantern, or a radish into the petals of a rose," but she also knows that he has his eccentricities: "He is afraid of the dark. He could not eat certain foods: sweet potato, cassava and tapioca" (206). He cannot talk about the things and events that remind him of the night he lost his father. Although he frequently has disturbing images and nightmares, Matthew is unable to articulate to himself or tell his wife and daughter about his traumatic memory, the horror of his experiences during the war. In her reading of *Certainty*, Y-Dang Troeung argues that although there is an impetus to "keep certain wounds open and alive in the public sphere...in order to combat historical erasure" (92), there are "psychic and material costs" to such acts (92). Troeung writes, "Thien's novel calls attention to these costs through an emphasis on the theme of return to trauma and on the necessity, sometimes, of forgetting" (92).

According to Thien, *Certainty*'s preoccupation with death and grief emerged because she wrote the novel shortly after her mother passed away. She says, "The only books I could read after she died were science books, a lot about the study of consciousness. I wanted to know, as a child does, where my mother went, what happened to that person" (qtd. in Scott, par. 4). She reveals her knowledge of trauma theory in a conversation between Gail and her husband, Ansel. Ansel talks about disassociation, where "the memories splinter into different worlds" (Thien 85). Gail reminds him that there is a biochemical element, too: "If there's a trauma, or a difficult memory, sometimes that severs the links. The memories themselves don't disappear, but you can't find your way back to them, because the glue that connects the different streams is somehow dissolved" (85). For many of the characters in the book, there is no complete healing. However, the narrative as a whole enables readers to connect, to make sense of various streams or different worlds, and to "remember" what we may have forgotten or not known. The text is like listening to the reels and reels of tapes Gail has made of people telling stories. She says, "Sometimes, people remember things they haven't thought about in years, a private memory, a story. You know that feeling when you're moving house, going through boxes, and you find something unexpected? That's what I feel is happening to them. Inside their minds, they open the box, and there it is right in front of them, almost as if they're seeing it for the first time" (84–85). Matthew, Ani, and Sipke's flashbacks bring alive for us many things, including the Sandakan Death Marches, which resulted in the deaths of more than six thousand civilian laborers and Allied prisoners of war held by the Empire of Japan. Landsberg notes, "The 'remembering' of particularly traumatic events of the collective past inevitably affects both the identity of the individual person and his or her previously accepted worldview. The 'strategic remembering' uniquely enabled by the technologies of mass culture has the power, then, to support a sense of collective social responsibility" (152).

The deaths of the past are connected to deaths of the characters who live in the present in Canada and the Netherlands. In the first few pages of the novel, one of the protagonists, Gail, is already dead. Even in contemporary society, her husband Ansel, who is a physician, is unable to save her from pneumonia. He regrets having failed to rush to her side when she first telephoned him to tell him she was ill. Gail's mother thinks, "the deepest pain comes from knowing that you are powerless, incapable of protecting the ones you love. A sudden death leaves so few answers. She and Matthew and Ansel are clutching at air, they are suspended in time" (129). Their sentiments are echoed by Sipke in the Netherlands: "When Ani died, his world had come to an end. In the days that followed, he sat in the living room, staring out at the canal, the great willows, and felt as if he, too, were passing into a kind of darkness" (234). While the novel is told "with a deep elegiac sense of life" (Cheuse) and there are many stories of deaths, the text is not depressing. Thien balances the uncertainties of life with a leitmotif of interconnectedness and patterns. Through the leitmotif, she suggests that events that seem to have no meaning nevertheless have a pattern when viewed from a different angle. At the dinner table in the first chapter of the book, Ansel talks about snowflakes, which are uniquely shaped by "changing weather conditions" (Thien 9). He argues, "Each addition to the crystal is dependent on the exact second of its formation, and its place in the atmosphere. Even a difference as small as a breath, or a nudge, will give rise to another shape, another sequence of order and complexity" (9). Later, a codebreaker expert, Jaarsma, talks about "the Mandelbrot Set": a corner of the picture is a "fractal image" and is similar to the entire picture (218). He points out that people, like birds that fly in a V formation, do not necessarily see the patterns they make, but the patterns are there: "the pattern that I cannot see, that I have no knowledge of, exists. My mind, my brain, is not made to imagine distances of great magnitude. Or infinite time, eternity. We glimpse a part of the puzzle and intimate, however vaguely, an answer" (219).

Ultimately, what these images suggest is that there is a web, a pattern that we are unable to see but that is there, unacknowledged. This belief is what distinguishes Thien's view from that of postmodernists, who tend to see disjunctions and disconnections without a sense of how pieces could fit together. Thien highlights sameness between people across the globe and even resorts to metaphysical conceits in order to make her point about the connections between life, animals, and the natural world. She draws examples from nature, such as snowflakes (9) and fish. Ani is told that each species of fish has "a distinctive sound" (153), and that one only needs to study the art of listening to hear them. She uses illustrations from medicine and neurology (X-rays and chemical synapses, 201), physics (Einstein and the speed of light, 118), and Bertrand Russell's philosophy (272) in order to show that "a kind of symmetry, not of left and right, but of large scales and small ones" (219), like the Mandelbrot Set, exists. Gail learns from Ansel that even an MRI scan has patterns that can reveal the "chemical traces of memory and love" (201), while Jaarsma tells her that the Mandelbrot Set, "one of the most complex objects in mathematics," is actually "a collection of points derived from the quadratic equation $z = z^2 + c$" (218). Even though not everything has a mathematical equation, each individual object, animal, or person fits relationally into a whole.

William Sullivan, who served in the Canadian army in Hong Kong during World War II and was taken prisoner by the Japanese, leaves a coded diary from a prisoner-of-war camp that functions as a nice mise en abyme for the novel. Instead of the great secrets Gail and his family expected, the diary reveals details of everyday life: "William Sullivan kept the diary as proof of a different kind of existence, where part of him still saw the world as if he were free. He wrote about their rituals, what time they got up in the morning, the kind of trees that grew outside the camp, the food they ate, the girl smugglers who passed by outside" (220–21). The entries are minutiae, but "through these sentences, these pages, he would make the world cohere" (221). His future is uncertain, but the concrete effort of recording his life helps him "maintain some part of his dignity" (221). Gail, reading the diary, thinks of Bertrand Russell, who believed that philosophy "was a means to teach one how to live without certainty, and yet without being paralyzed by hesitation" (273).

In the end, there are no great revelations or secrets to be uncovered. But in both *Gangster* and *Certainty*, the particulars of the everyday, the constant rejuvenation and transformation that nature affords, enable people to survive the precarity that comes from traumatic memories, to forget their losses and make sense of their lives.

CHAPTER 4

Representations of Aging
in Asian Canadian Performance

> Life is not a series of gig lamps
> symmetrically arranged; life is a
> luminous halo, a semi-transparent
> envelope surrounding us from the
> beginning of consciousness to the
> end.
>
> —Virginia Woolf, "Modern Fiction"

Our contemporary society views aging as an inevitable process characterized by a series of losses, by the slow decline of powers and prowess, and by the diminution of physical, mental skills, and cognitive function. In a world where beauty and ability are associated with the young, the aged are constantly urged to battle their bodily changes through makeup, medicine, surgery, and other kinds of treatments. Anthropologist Peter Stephenson writes, "As an impediment, age has become commoditized, brokered, commercialized, and the principal object of a vast system of health-care practices that make the elderly the primary target of the political economy of aging" (4, paraphrasing Stephen Katz). He calls our society today a "culture of novelty" with its emphasis on "'youth culture' in marketing and the major industries of the self which focus on the body in consumer culture—cosmetics, clothing, and many forms of health care associated with the 'anti-aging' movement" (4). These industries, he says, are "an unfailing index of the importance of individuated forms of newness or novelty" (4). To be old, in short, is to be a failure, someone to be pitied, tolerated, humored, or ignored.

In contrast to this view of aging is the veneration of the old among some non-Western and nonmodern cultures, such as Aboriginal and Asian. Aging

and elders in these cultures are associated with wisdom, with insights and experiences accumulated over time. In both Chinese and Japanese societies, Confucian principles of filial piety, the practice of respecting and caring for one's
parents in their old age, have been used recurrently in history as a basis of social
order, spiritual anchoring, moral conduct, and social control (Hashimoto and
Ikels, 437). Akiko Hashimoto and Charlotte Ikels note, "Historically, respect
for elders has been an integral part of the practice of ancestor reverence in the
traditional family systems in East Asia. In the moral order of the 'traditional'
family, the elderly held higher spiritual status with advancing age" (437). Stephenson contends that in Western culture, "what is conventionally termed
'the aging process' is especially constrained in both biological and cultural
arenas by a notion of linear time still firmly rooted in a now discredited kind
of Newtonian physics, which lends it an aura of constancy and universality"
(10). According to Stephenson,

> Time is conventionally understood as quantifiable and delimited—a "thing"
> that can be "spent," "saved," and "lost"; indeed, it is frequently "invested."
> "Time is money" is a common phrase, so time can be said to have assumed
> the status of virtual currency in a temporal commodities market that now
> operates globally. Time and money are both employed as finite measures, so
> time is comprehended as a material commodity. If we accept that time is a
> commodity, then it follows that it is produced.... This kind of time is prob-
> ably crucial to the development of industrial societies as a means of ordering
> events and controlling labour. It is monochromatic in the sense that it in-
> volves doing only one thing at a time in repeating calendrical sequences. (11)

Time is seen as a linear movement as we imagine ourselves "moving forward,
inevitably, until we reach an end," whereas in "many societies where time has
a more eternal presence—a 'now-ness' about it—aging also has a qualitatively
different feel" (12).

This chapter looks at two contemporary texts by Asian Canadians that deal
with aging and the aged. I look at important ways in which filmmaker Linda
Ohama and performer/playwright Catherine Hernandez contest popular Western notions of aging by focusing on affective memories that forestall linear time.
Instead of representing the aged woman's body through industrial or postin-
dustrial metaphors of "breakdown" and wearing out (Stephenson 18), Ohama
and Hernandez emphasize qualities such as energy and endurance in their
female protagonists. Through the use of flashbacks, memories, magic realism,
and motifs, these authors challenge not only the cultural view of the aged and
aging but also our experience of time and our understanding of how history
is handled. This chapter differs from the others in my book because it focuses

not on youths and working-age immigrants but on those whom society customarily sees as beyond visual and narrative interest, those who are beyond the age of economic and professional productivity. But the aged, like young Asian North Americans, can experience feelings of depression and precarity. The Administration on Aging estimates that more than 1.3 million Asian, Hawaiian, and Pacific Islander individuals were aged sixty-five and older in 2008, and this figure is projected to grow to over 7.6 million by 2050. In Canada, as in other developed countries, the aging population is "expected to present significant social, economic and political challenges over the next decades" (Kembhavi). By 2041, seniors are "projected to comprise nearly a quarter (24.5%) of the Canadian population." In 2012, immigrants, mostly born in Western Europe and Asia, made up 28% of the senior population (Kembhavi). Yet there are still relatively few works of literature devoted to senior Asian North Americans.

In our clock-watching culture, we are used to waking up, eating, and working according to time and for certain periods of time. Even leisurely activities, such as exercising or going to see a film, are timed—for example, we make ourselves exercise for twenty minutes or watch a film that is ninety minutes long. Yet Stephenson argues that time itself, like history, is a cultural construct that we have created and become accustomed to. Some drugs, for example analgesic drug therapies, can alter the "embodied experience of linear time" (18). He notes, "Time isn't something 'out there' in the first place; it is a product of the same system that anaesthetics shut down" (18). With "anaesthetics, the experience is one where time collapses completely and we are not aware of its 'passing' at all. . . . Time can be experienced as a tempo: slow or fast; it can expand and contract, or we can even experience ourselves outside it altogether when our self—our identity—is deeply absorbed in the moment. This can also be understood as a characteristic of persons who have become contemplative, quiet, adapted, and serene and focused on the present, rather than the unknowable future" (18).

Unarticulated Emotions in *Obaachan's Garden*

In the lives of people on vacation, retired people, and older folks, time often loses its sense of urgency. In *Obaachan's Garden* (2001), Japanese Canadian Linda Ohama's biographical documentary film about her grandmother Asayo Murakami, historical time, with its emphasis on dates and locations, is juxtaposed with the grandmother's accounts of her life, those moments of affect. While the narrator presents dates, such as 1923, when Tokyo was hit by an earthquake of a great magnitude, and 1924, when Obaachan comes to Canada as a picture bride, Obaachan herself seems no longer to depend on dates as life markers. On her one-hundredth birthday in 1998, the family gets ready for a celebration. However, Obaachan does not attend her own birthday party, and they end up celebrating it later. She fails to perform the role that is expected of her on her birthday, refusing to be feted and fussed over. Instead of clocks and calendars, what marks the passing of time in the film are repetitive acts and images that show other ways of denoting historical changes. Some of these scenes or vignettes include the pounding of rice dough for traditional sweet cakes, the planting of flowers in Obaachan's lush and colorful garden, and the making and bottling of sake. These motifs tend to stress repetition and continuity rather than linear progression. In addition, Ohama uses an interesting technique to focus on the figure of the aged woman at the same time as she is able to make her life story come alive. She returns again and again to her grandmother as the central narrator, using her voice-over in Japanese while showing black-and-white footage from documentaries or newsreels, combined with re-enactments of highlights from Obaachan's life. We never forget whose story this is, and that these are what Maria Sturken has called "embodied memories" (34).

Literary scholar Sally Chivers has looked at the way contemporary Canadian writers have refigured older women's bodies, deconstructing "ill-considered, socially damaging prejudices toward a visible, usually disenfranchised, minority" (xiii). Disability scholar Rosemarie Thomson has pointed out the "constructed identity" of "the normate," a figure who, by "way of the bodily configurations and cultural capital they assume, can step into a position of authority and wield the power it grants them" (8). The aged body, like the disabled body, is seen as lacking, frail, and imperfect vis-à-vis the "normate," the healthy, young, abled body in our society. I want to continue Chivers's and Thomson's critiques of social assumptions and stereotypes about the aged but with a different focus. I am interested in the way memories, particularly affective ones, can shape our understanding of both a person's life and the measure of time in that life. By affective memories, I mean those memories of past events that aroused an affective response in the subject, not only during the time when the events were taking place but also at a later moment, in recollections of the events. In the diegesis of a narrative, whether it be a film or a play, the representation of affective moments often arouses anew the affects that were present in the initial encounter.

Affect has been described as those experiences that elicit a bodily reaction that exceeds linguistic representation. Following Brian Massumi, Eric Shouse defines affect as "a nonconscious experience of intensity; it is a moment of unformed and unstructured potential. . . . Affect is the body's way of preparing itself for action in a given circumstance by adding a quantitative dimension to the intensity of the quality of an experience" (par. 5). He distinguishes between feeling, emotion, and affect: "Feelings are *personal* and *biographical*, emotions are *social*, and affects are *prepersonal*" (par. 2). Feeling is "personal and biographical because every person has a distinct set of previous sensations from which to draw when interpreting and labelling their feelings" (par. 3), while "[a]n emotion is the projection/display of a feeling" . . . that "can be either genuine or feigned" (par 4). Virginia Demos notes that affects can involve "the facial muscles, the viscera, the respiratory system, the skeleton, autonomic blood flow changes, and vocalisations that act together to produce an analogue of the particular gradient or intensity of stimulation impinging on the organism" (qtd. in Shouse par. 6). These moments of affect, moments of intense joy, excitement, anger, fear, or disgust, are at once "all powerful and powerless" in our daily lives (Greil Marcus, qtd. in Seigworth 20). In many cases, they are those unforgettable moments where we feel we have lived keenly, in a manner somewhat like Virginia Woolf's "moments of being."[1] While we cannot control when these moments occur in life, a playwright or filmmaker can choose to highlight these moments in an elderly protagonist's life in order to represent his or her vital aspects and to counter the expectations of fraility or helplessness generated by the visual image of the aging body.

In *Obaachan's Garden*, the tension between feelings that are expressed and those that cannot be articulated through language is particularly intense. Through the course of her interviews with her grandmother, Linda Ohama unearths a secret Obaachan has not disclosed to her husband or their eight Japanese Canadian children, who were all born after she moved to Canada. Before her one-hundredth birthday, Obaachan reveals to her extended family in Canada that she was previously married in Japan, and that in that first marriage she bore three children: two girls, Fumiko and Chieko, and a son who died shortly after birth. The disclosure of her first family explains why she appears not entirely happy in her life, and why her children feel that she is unable to give them unconditional love. Even when she is surrounded by her large family, there is always a kind of darkness about her, which Linda Ohama's mother (Obaachan's daughter) notices. Linda's mother says, for example, that "there was always something that she didn't share with us." Obaachan does not seem to have many tangible traces of this former life: her only record of her first marriage and its children seems to be a few photographs she has of the two daughters, photographs she cherishes and takes out periodically to look at.

---

1. In "A Sketch of the Past," Virginia Woolf distinguishes between moments in which she experiences life intensely and those moments of "non being" when we are not conscious of our lives but simply doing routine things: "one walks, eats, sees things, deals with what has to be done" (1214).

Having past experiences she cannot discuss with the people she interacts with daily presents an interesting way of studying responses to particular affects, as affects are also about unconscious bodily responses, often unarticulated.

Shame is one of the affects that Obaachan carries with her from Japan to Canada. Linda Ohama finds out that the reason Obaachan abandoned those two daughters in Tokyo is that Obaachan and her first husband's family did not get along. When the third baby, a boy, died shortly after his birth, the husband's family saw Obaachan as a failure as wife and mother because of her inability to bear heirs, and they removed her from the family. Sara Ahmed says that "shame can be described as an intense and painful sensation that is bound up with how the self feels about itself, a self-feeling that is felt by and on the body. Certainly, when I feel shame, I have done something that I feel is bad" (*Politics* 103). For this reason, Obaachan hides her past from her Canadian family for over seventy-five years, a sign that she must have felt great shame and pain about the whole experience. The sense of shame at having failed to produce a son for her first husband also explains why she was later so eager to bring George, her first son with her second husband, back to Japan to show him off.

The fact that she has kept her first marriage a secret from her Canadian family means that she is unable to share her pain and her anxieties about Fumiko and Chieko, whom she left behind at six and four, with anyone in Canada. Even though she has been away from Japan and from her first two daughters for decades, she thinks about them and remembers them often, walking seven miles when she expects to get mail from her sister in Japan. One poignant moment in the film occurs right after Obaachan and her husband hear of the bombing of Hiroshima during the Second World War, a war that led to the internment of Japanese Canadians, including Obaachan's family. Feeling helpless and frustrated, the husband lashes out, while Obaachan is overwhelmed with fear and grief. Believing her daughters to be in the vicinity of Hiroshima, Obaachan can express her anxiety and her pain only through her music. Ohama depicts her grandmother's anguish and distress through sound and visual imagery: the discordant notes of the violin, the woman running and crying distraughtly from the civilized indoor domestic setting to the prairie fields outside. The scene of Obaachan in the fields is interjected with cuts of her memories of her little girls and newsreel footage of the victims of the nuclear bomb, depicting her memories and her imagined fears about the girls.

Ohama's mise-en-scène of the scene of affect intensifies the affective response of the viewers. The dramatization of Obaachan's recollection of this moment is stagy and hyperbolic, recalling King Lear's distress. The setting of the fields of wheat and the posture of the pliant woman may also bring to mind

Andrew Wyeth's *Christina's World*. Although the scene is not played in slow motion, there is a slow quality about it, a prolonging of the moment of anguish that stops linear time. This is one of those moments where affect and memory stop time, where words and linguistic communication become inadequate and superfluous. I suggest that scenes like these, which depict affective responses and memories of the aged, help create an awareness of the rich emotional life of older people. Embedding an affective experience within an institutional time of calendars—nursing home schedules—changes the qualitative experience of Obaachan and those around her. Memories do not stop time literally, but they can expand and slow down clock time by making one feel more intensely. Through such moments in the film, we see Obaachan no longer just as the old woman in a wheelchair but as someone strong who has endured and triumphed.

Personal Anecdote: Pleasurable Memories

This scene from *Obaachan's Garden* is of an affective memory that is unforgettable because of its pain and anguish. Affective memories can also be joyful. Before moving on to my second example, I want to give a personal anecdote about an affective memory that also seemed to have momentarily stopped time. It occured in 2010, a couple of months before my mother passed away. At that time, my mother (then seventy-nine), was living in a nursing home and had limited mobility. She walked with the help of a walker, and her arthritic pains made every day a struggle. Often, she was reluctant to go anywhere because displacement was such an effort. On this particular Saturday evening, I persuaded her to come home with me and have dinner with my family. I picked her up from the nursing home and brought her home with me. Even though I made her her favorite noodles, she barely ate anything, complaining of pains in her hip, her knees, and elsewhere. After dinner, she wanted to go back to the nursing home to "lie down."

It was still early, so I invited her to sit on our family room sofa while I washed the dishes. My eldest son happened to be transferring home videos from VHS to DVD. They were videos of our children and family from some ten years back, and my mother appeared in many of the family events—birthday parties, outings, vacations, and trips. My mother in the videos was a much more agile and energetic self. In spite of her pain and her tiredness, my mother began to watch these videos with interest. My children were also watching, and they said, "There you are, Ama, you were babysitting us. You even came on a hike with us.... Look, you picked me up.... Look how strong you were." Sure enough, there were videos of my mother and my children playing together in the backyard, going on a canoe trip, and going for a hike. She remarked, "I was very brave to do that," with amazement and disbelief at a younger image of herself on the screen. Unconsciously, her face changed from misery to pleasure as she watched herself carrying my toddlers, playing with the kids, and rolling and frying a hundred spring rolls for a family gathering. For approximately two hours, we heard no moans, nothing of her pains. It was just pleasant memories, smiles, and laughter as we watched these home movies. We had a lovely evening, reminiscing about the past and about how sweet the kids were when they were younger. It was one of the last few evenings that I remember her being in such a good mood.

Later I drove her back to her nursing home. As soon as we reached the entrance with its fluorescent lights and automatic doors, she said, "Ow," and complained of her pains again. She was having difficulty moving her legs to get out of the car. The funny thing was, I had not heard her moan for a while. Then I remembered the present time and the reality of her aging body once again. This incident led me to think about the ways affective memories can suspend bodily pain. It seemed to me that for two hours, as we were watching those videos that brought back pleasant memories, time was on hold. Is it possible to fill one's time with pleasant memories that can change the shape and texture of one's body and one's life in the present? The incident suggests that affective memories have power not only over one's psychic and emotional state but also over one's physical well-being.

Staging Affect in *Eating with Lola*

In the example from *Obaachan's Garden*, the representation of Obaachan's shame about her past and her emotional recollection of the bombings in Hiroshima helped fill out the contours of an aged woman's life, transforming the elderly woman into a subject who has a history and who merits our attention and interest. In the example of my mother, affective memories seem to be able to suspend time and even bodily pain, albeit temporarily. With my third and last example, I want to suggest that happy memories can similarly reconfigure our perception of the sick body to one of strength and beauty, creating interest in a figure that would usually not excite notice. In Filipino Canadian Catherine Hernandez's performance *Eating with Lola* (2010), the seemingly ill grandmother (*Lola* means "grandmother" in Filipino) metamorphoses into a desirable young woman through the performer's voice and singing. In this case, unlike in the documentary film, the flashbacks are rendered aurally rather than visually.

The play is a one-woman puppet show with Catherine Hernandez manipulating a small Muppet-like puppet. She says of the piece, "*Eating with Lola* began as an obituary" to her maternal grandmother, Lola Pacing: "Typical of most children of migrant Filipinos, I had only seen my Lola four times when I had the chance to visit Manila and in those fleeting moments, she still was a mystery. . . . The play was [born] out of the fantasy of being given the chance to actually be my Lola's grandchild. Be in the room with her. Be beside her and nurse her" ("Eating with Puppets"). The performance consists of only one woman on stage with a puppet, which represents Lola. The other characters are represented by a "series of props that draws on vocal mask" (Hernandez, *Eating with Lola* "Playwright's notes"). The Lola character puppet is made of soft material, similar to Jim Henson's Muppets. Characterization comes mainly from Hernandez's skill in acting, speech accents, body movements, and strategic use of a few props. A workshop performance of the play was staged at fu-GEN Asian Canadian Theatre's Potluck Festival on May 8, 2010, in Toronto. Hernandez uses simple props such as hats, sunglasses, a handkerchief, and a cigarette to distinguish between a number of characters.

On the use of puppets, Tzachi Zamir notes that "puppets enable slowing down emotion, . . . breaking down emotional expression into discrete units, . . . to represent by embodying a fragment of a larger whole" (407). He explains:

> The puppet's resistance to embodying realistic projections, its dissimilarity from actors and the inner processes that the latter appear to disclose, transports it into the sphere of partial similitude. Here our predilection to favor mimetic acting, the kind of acting that would enable us to perceive characters as people, may obstruct our capacity to relate to the specific language of partial characterization embodied in puppetry. . . .
> . . . The puppet, by contrast, is internally dead and externally alive. The imagination in this instance does not merely fill out a missing picture but rather allows itself to be affected by what it acknowledges to be a void shrouded by expression. The amusement and laughter that puppets typically invoke can point to the uncanny nature of the content of this art form, playing as it does on the boundaries between lifelessness and life. (407, 409)

This ability to communicate emotions makes the puppet ideally suited to convey and create affect. The fact that we do not seek verisimilitude when we watch a puppet show enables a puppeteer/performer to make the puppet as old or as young as she wants or to condense time. Through the puppet, Hernandez is able to shift the grandmother from lifelessness to life very quickly through synecdoche.

As its title suggests, food and cooking play primary roles in *Eating with Lola*. Food functions as a prompt for the evocation of memories, and it creates tension between the grandmother and her granddaughter. When the play begins, the finicky grandmother rejects nineteen-year-old Grace's attempts to cook food for her. Now eighty-seven, Lola feels she has become a burden to her family, whereas she used to be the "best cook around" when she was younger. Grace brings her sleeping grandmother (her Lola) some food. The old woman's stillness and unresponsiveness make Grace think that she is dead, but she is just grumpy and not interested in tasteless "baby food." To show her granddaughter that she "wasn't always like this," the grandmother starts telling her about how great she was not only at cooking but in the tasks "of getting food, of finding food, of stealing food." The flashback to when Lola was a young woman is created by simple but effective elements. Lola the puppet puts a flower in her hair, and her voice transforms into that of a teenager, singing "Ain't Misbehavin.'" Instantly, the puppet appears to have become young. As Lola the puppet tells the story of her past, she appears to gather strength, beauty, and youthfulness. Lola tells Grace of her resourcefulness. Her family circumstances during the Japanese occupation of the Philippines were awful, as there was little food, but Lola narrates her intrepid and enterprising efforts with some pride. Lola was just sixteen and working for a bar that catered to American GIs stationed in Manila right after the Liberation of the Philippines from Japanese occupation. Lola remembers not only the flirtatious soldiers who invited her out but also how she had to "find leftovers" to bring home for herself, her six brothers and sisters, and her mother. From the bar she was able to bring home empty cans of Spam, corned beef, and ketchup for her family, scraping out the edges and sides of the can to feed them. She also became cook for an American woman, and she occasionally skimmed off the bottom of steaks to feed her siblings. The telling of this story transforms Lola from a bedridden old woman to a brave and spunky young woman. Her cooking skills, especially her ability to make delicious *pianono* (a jelly roll cake filled with custard), made her invaluable to her employer and made a famous war hero, Manuel Sanchez, fall in love with her.

In the flashback narratives, Lola is transformed from an old lady into someone young, desirable, and capable. In addition to food references, Hernandez uses songs and music to change the mood, re-creating the enchantment of the romance between her grandmother and Manuel, a legendary spy and radio operator. Marriage, motherhood, familial life, and Manuel's death of a heart attack all in the space of a decade are condensed into a few vignettes, but they enable Grace and the audience to feel Lola's nostalgia, wonder, and sense of regret for lost youth and possibilities. We see Lola no longer as a bedridden, ill woman but as she was in her prime. The details about her cooking, for example, making "the perfect *torta*" using the wooden spoon Manuel carved for her, render her a palpable character and endear her to us. These flashbacks convey a sense of Lola's passion, as well as her inventiveness and resourcefulness as she cooks and tries to feed her many brothers and sisters with the excesses, remnants, and discards from the kitchens of her various employers. Yet the sentimentality of the past is undercut by the contrapuntal presence of Grace, who did not appreciate Lola's cooking as a child. In a later flashback, when Lola shows Grace an *ube-macapuno* cake she made for the girl's tenth birthday, Grace runs away, saying, "It's gross, Lola. It's blue. It looks like it's rotten." Grace's childish reaction to the non-Western food her grandmother prepares raises issues of cultural difference and ethnic assimilation in the younger generation. Lola's cooking is too reminiscent of old ways and the old country for her Americanized granddaughter.

Aside from demonstrating the disjunction of sensibilities between grandmother and granddaughter, the flashback scenes also blur the boundaries between what Maurice Halbwachs has termed "autobiographical" and "historical" memory. Halbwachs has argued that autobiographical memory is "memory of events that we have personally experienced in the past," while historical memory can be reached only "through written records and other types of records, such as photography" (as paraphrased by Coser, 23–24). Through the grandmother's storytelling, Grace and audience members learn of some Filipino acts of heroism during the Japanese occupation, acts that are usually found in oral history or in asides in history books. Martin Ponce, citing Luis Taruc's *Born of the People* (1953), notes that the United States did not acknowledge the work of Filipino guerrillas in the Second World War. "What happened in 1945 was almost a duplication of what had happened in 1898. The American army, on both occasions, landed to find a revolutionary movement fighting against the common enemy. On both occasions they took steps to crush it, and on both occasions they found allies in the exploiting classes of Filipinos" (Taruc 274–75, qtd. in Ponce 103). However, after the war, many of those who fought in the underground resistance—including Taruc, who led a large people's army against the Japanese invaders in World War II—were credited not as heroes but as rebels. In the performance, Grace's grandfather Manuel worked as a repairman at a Manila hotel that became one of the Japanese headquarters, so he was able to spy on the Japanese for the Americans. However, Japanese soldiers discovered him and tortured him for seven days, removing his toenails. His act of resistance is incorporated into Lola's narrative of her whirlwind romance, which creates sympathy for a character who appears only briefly on stage. His tale of survival, like other tales of Filipino resistance, is part of Philippine history, but in *Eating with*

Lola, the story becomes part of Lola's fictionalized autobiographical memory, a recollection that arouses an affective response in her listeners and transforms autobiographical memory into part of our collective memory.

While Ohama uses a combination of first-person narration, documentary footage, and dramatic re-enactment to tell a version of her grandmother's story, Hernandez acts, manipulates the puppet, and uses a dramatic voice to create a range of emotions from anger and pain to joy and love. She is able to switch from one emotional state to another quickly, shifting from past to present and from youth to age by the use of simple props. Time is more easily compressed into a small space. Unwilling to be a burden or to be pitied, Hernandez's Lola is feisty and willful to the end, refusing to follow her doctor's orders to eat bland foods and to sit still, even after she has a stroke. It is her pugnacious nature that makes Lola enchanting and difficult as a character. Hernandez's simulation of how doctors and nurses treat old people in nursing homes creates humor in the play but also arouses compassion for the elderly and the feeble. When Lola falls ill and is placed in a home, she says, "I can't really describe what it felt like to be inside there. . . . Not a nightmare. More like a movie that never wants to end. Just watching, not doing." The caregivers and doctors around her infantilize her:

> Hello Rufina. Can you follow my finger? Can you see it? Good. Follow it. Good. Do you know what day it is? Mrs. Sanchez, you've just had a stroke. Can you feel this side of your body? Good morning. Lift up your arm. Can you squeeze my hand for me? Excellent. Good afternoon. Time to change your bags, Mrs. Sanchez. Good night. Lights out, okay?

When she comes back to live with her family, she is also unable to achieve the dignity she wishes. In a dramatic scene toward the end of the performance, Lola attempts to cook her own food in spite of her family's instructions that she stay in bed and simply heat fast food in the microwave. For Lola, cooking has long been a matter of pride and skill. In her old age, her inability to cook for herself is symptomatic of her degeneration. In one scene that is acted out silently except for the occasional grunt, Lola is left alone in the house. She gets up, puts in her teeth, and shuffles slowly to the kitchen by holding on to one piece of furniture after another. She tastes the fast food left by her family in the fridge but spits it out with disgust. Then, she slowly makes herself something fresh, a torta with onions, garlic, eggs, and ground beef. However, Lola is unable to enjoy the wonderful-smelling torta. Just as she is about to take her first bite, a crumb of beef falls to the ground. Lola attempts to clean the floor with a cloth, and bending down, she falls to the ground in pain. It is a moving scene, as Lola's attempt at independence and defiance ends in defeat, illness, and apparent failure.

Like Ohama's scene of grief, this scene elicits affective responses without using language. Through the puppet's exaggerated gestures we experience grief for this aged, frail body who is still mentally and spiritually strong. Zamir writes, "In its structure and artistic medium, the resisting puppet crystallizes a more fraught sense of the body; the body that should have been a transparent, expressive tool, a frictionless vehicle of agency, becomes visible, annoying, limiting, and free. For its spectators, the puppet can thus integrate the opposites of body and soul, resisting matter and expressed volition, the vexing freedom of flesh, and the friction involved in controlling one's roles as they become autonomous" (393). Lola collapses before us, and we watch her transform from a body of strength to a helpless one in a matter of seconds. Time, too, seems to collapse as we experience Lola's moment of triumph disintegrate into one of failure. As spectators, we experience intense sadness because in our minds we contrast the strong woman who was a fantastic cook with the one who is now unable to pick up a crumb from the floor. Past and present coexist simultaneously in the puppet's body in this scene.

Finally, in both *Obaachan's Garden* and *Eating with Lola*, there is a strong conjunction between personal time and historical time. In her study of *Obaachan's Garden* and Ann Marie Fleming's film *The Magical Life of Long Tack Sam*, Rocío Davis writes of the importance of these kinds of family documentaries as they "mediate history in three ways: first, through the recovery and safeguarding of family stories from historical erasure; second, by entering into a dialogue with official or public histories; and, third, by proposing cultural forms for present and future communities" (4). What Davis says about Ohama's and Fleming's films applies to Hernandez's work as well: "they serve an important didactic purpose by introducing transnational history and the history of immigration to mainstream or ethnic Canadians, inviting them to consider the processes that created particular ethnic communities. Because the content of Asian Canadian narration generally involves racialization, social experience, and political engagement, the narrative becomes 'history'—the public story of a past shared with others" (4). While my analysis focuses on aging rather than the production of history, here, following Davis, I want to note that these works contribute to what Maurice Halbwachs has called "collective memory" (22). Lewis Coser notes, "Every collective memory requires the support of a group delimited in space and time" (22). The past, as constructed in history, often omits the stories and roles of women during times of upheaval and war, focusing instead on national leaders, war heroes, and politics. By enacting the stories of their grandmothers' pasts, these works create a supportive group to remember these women's histories.

On the use of personal memories, Marita Sturken notes,

> When personal memories are deployed in the context of marking the an-niversary of historical events, they are presented as either the embodied evidence of history or as evidence of history's failures. Survivors return to the sites of their war experience; they place their bodies within the discourse of remembering to either affirm history's narratives or to declare them in-complete, incapable of conjuring their experience. They represent a very particular form of embodied memory. . . .
>
> . . . At the same time, the tension of history and memory problematizes this very question of experience. The original experiences of memory are irre-trievable; we cannot ever "know" them except through memory remains. . . . Memory is ontologically fluid and memories constantly subject to re-scripting and fantasy. This does not mean that we cannot address issues of authenticity and accuracy in memory, but that we must foreground memory's relationship to desire and its political nature. Indeed, what memories tell us, more than anything, is about the stakes held by individuals and institutions in what the past means. (34)[2]

In highlighting the turmoil and displacement experienced by women during such historical events as World War II, the internment of Japanese Canadians and the occupation of Manila by the Japanese, both Ohama and Hernandez enable us to become aware of what is memorialized and what is left out of history. By re-creating events that conflate personal and historical events, the authors present us with a fuller understanding of history. By foregrounding the aged bodies of their grandmothers and by using affective memories, they refocus our attention to bodies that our society often ignores or sees as failed, at the same time as they suggest the possibility of reconfiguring the linear way we experience and measure time.

---

2. Sturken studies Rhea Tajiri's film *History and Memory* (1991) in the context of other Hollywood films such as *Bataan* (1943), *Sands of Iwo Jima* (1949), and *Gung Ho!* (1944) and argues that Tajiri's film "reenacts the absent presence of the Japanese American in-ternment" (40).

Work, Depression, Failure

In the last chapter, I examined how negative notions of old age and time were transformed and reconfigured in art through a film and a puppet performance. This chapter looks at repercussions of the sense of failure in two stories of second-generation Asian immigrant women who grew up assimilated into North American culture and became successful professionals but who experience a crisis and fall into depression. Mimi, a character in Catherine Hernandez's play *Singkil* (2009), and journalist Jan Wong both suffer from a breakdown that forces them to rethink or reassess their priorities and identities. *Singkil* is, in part, a coming-of-age story, while *Out of the Blue* (2012) is "a memoir of workplace depression" (cover). Though different in genre, these two works recount Asianfails that critique the model minority discourse, and they also show the links between private health and professional, social trauma. The illness or death of a family member becomes a catalyst for uncovering family histories and buried memories, which in turn lead to questions about the unreasonable expectations and pressures experienced by Asian North Americans.

Affect and the Past in *Singkil*

In M. J. Kang's *Noran Bang: The Yellow Room*, the death of a grandmother in Korea gives rise to a series of memories and flashbacks about a Korean Canadian family's preimmigration period, when the whole family was together in Korea.

The threat of death or serious illness often reminds one of mortality and family secrets. The first part of this chapter examines Catherine Hernandez's play *Singkil* and its use of the past, which arouses an affective response from Mimi, the twenty-something female protagonist. "Affect," as Michael Hardt reminds us, draws attention to the body and emotions as well as to the mind: "affect straddles these two divides: between the mind and body, and between actions and passions" (xi). Affect suggests a correspondence between "the mind's power to think and the body's power to act, and between the power to act and the power to be affected" (xi). In *Singkil* and *Eating with Lola*, an affective response to a mother's or grandmother's past life enables the young protagonists, women in twenty-first-century North America, to better understand themselves and offers them a way out of their depression or seemingly failed lives.

Though different in genre, the two plays are similar in depicting a young adult exploring untold stories of the older generation of immigrants. The narrative device of using two or three generations is not new to Asian North American authors. The best-known example of this kind of storytelling is Amy Tan's *Joy Luck Club*, which made popular the stories of four Chinese women in pre-1949 China and their American-born daughters in California. The stories of the older generation reveal the complex weaving of sociopolitical history with the personal. Lisa Lowe has praised Tan's novel as one that reveals the "heterogeneity of Chinese-American family relations" because it depicts "different examples of mother-daughter discord and concord" (35, 36). However, it has also been criticized as reductive, exoticizing China and Chinatown life. Sau-ling Wong writes, "Tan subsumes every element of Chinatown life into a drama of East-West confrontation, only this time with the Chinese prevailing. What the Chinese mothers do in the course of their mothering is always heavily fraught with cultural significance. Being bearers of traditional Chinese values appears to be their only preoccupation and occupation: as what might be called 'professional ethnic mothers,' they are constantly demonstrating some ancestral wisdom or other to their daughters, and indirectly to the readers" ("Ethnic Subject" 257). In her essay, Wong discusses the difficulty of depicting "authentic Chinese traditions, without falling into the trap of exoticization and playing into ahistorical essentialism" (254).

Twenty-some years after *The Joy Luck Club*, questions about ethnic identity and representation are still crucial. Authors and artists of color still find it difficult to portray their experiences and ethnic practices without being seen as representative of a particular culture. David Palumbo-Liu notes, "Minority cultures, that is, those cultures which have been marked as differing significantly from what is construed to be the dominant culture, have always had a particularly problematic relationship to the concept of the universal: the dominant has declared itself *as* universal, the quality of universality in turn is affirmed as the pre-requisite for anything seeking entrance into the dominant culture" ("Universalism" 188). As a writer, theater practitioner, and educator, Catherine Hernandez is aware of the issues surrounding ethnic cultural productions. In a comment about the state of theater in Toronto, she says:

> As a theatre artist of colour, I think there's a lot to be excited about and yet we have a long way to go. I remember interviewing filmmaker Midi Onadera when I was starting out as a journalist and I asked her what her thoughts were on the Reel Asian Film Festival. She told me she was thrilled it existed and yet sad it existed. Thrilled because it meant that Asians have a voice and yet sad that the festival had to exist in order for them to have a voice. It's the same way I feel about the blossoming of fu-GEN Asian Canadian Theatre Company. I look forward to the day that we needn't be ghettoized in order for our stories to be told. ("State of Theatre")

She feels it is important to strike a balance between the universal and the particular:

> Right now, the Asian-Canadian theatre community is experiencing an interesting shift in storytelling, and I would like to be part of that wave. Basically, we are moving on from the usual immigrant identity story and trying to move to more universal themes that happen to be framed by a specific cultural lattice. This is particularly important to me since it gives me the freedom to make my work less autobiographical, then I have more flexibility with my storylines and how they develop.

Thus, in her works, Hernandez deals with universal themes of anger, familial discord, mourning, love, and forgiveness, but she uses cultural references that are specific to the Filipino community. In her plays, characters are usually Filipino, but they are not burdened with being the bearers of authentic Filipino or Southeast Asian culture. As part of the group that Min Hyoung Song calls the "children of 1965," Hernandez does not necessarily write according to our expectations of an "Asian American" writer, but her works help "readers think imaginatively about what the near future holds for a country on the cusp of dramatic changes to its demographic composition, geopolitical prominence, and environmental well-being" (11). Her plays and performances elicit affective responses from the audience by appealing to a wide range of emotions that are not necessarily specific to Asian Canadian or Filipino culture. In his study *Beyond the Nation*, Martin Ponce also emphasizes the need to explore the "heterogeneity" within diasporic Filipino literature, to emphasize "its internal differences but also its outward connections to other(s') traditions and practices" (223).

Singkil explores a number of issues pertinent to people in their twenties, some of which are related to being Filipina Canadian, but many of which are not. In the play, first staged at the Factory Theatre in Toronto in 2007, the past is a secretive and fraught space filled with betrayal and confusion. After her mother's death, Mimi finds a headpiece from her mother's dance costume. This object and the arrival of her mother's long-lost friend from the Philippines propel Mimi into a journey of healing and self-discovery, enabling her to better understand her Filipino culture, her estranged parents, and her anger. The play is important because it explores topics that are not usually talked about in Asian North American families: depression, infidelity, and matrophobia. Hernandez, director Nina Lee Aquino, and designer Camellia Koo use devices such as staged flashbacks, a raised platform with hidden compartments, conflated identities between the mother and the daughter, and the enactment of folkloric narrative. These devices all enable Hernandez to reveal the entangled web of connections between home, history, memory, fantasy, nostalgia, and belonging in the diasporic subject.

Hernandez's play is interesting because it tells the story of two generations of Filipino Canadian women: Maria, who immigrated to Canada in the 1970s to join her husband, and her daughter Mimi, a second-generation frustrated and confused young woman who suffers from depression. For Mimi and also for her mother, the past cannot be viewed without an excessive charge of emotion and unease. Feelings of uncertainty and disappointment cloud their thoughts about the past, and they are unable to talk about certain events they experienced. This inability to communicate cripples them both. According to Sara Ahmed, "the word 'emotion' comes from Latin, *emovere*, referring to 'to move, to move out'. So emotions are what move us. But emotions are also *about* attachments, about what connects us to this or that. The relationship between movement and attachment is instructive. What moves us, what makes us feel, is also that which holds us in place, or gives us a dwelling place" ("Collective" 27). In her article "Collective Feelings," Ahmed argues that "emotions do things, and work to align individuals with collectives—or bodily space with social space—through the very intensity of their attachments" (26). However, the obverse is also true. Feeling the wrong emotions or feeling a lack of emotion when a collective expects one to feel a certain way can distance one from a social space or a collective. When the individual does not experience the same affective responses as the social body, he or she feels alienated from the community.

In *Singkil*, the main female protagonist, Mimi, has been moving from one high-paying job to another. In the three years after college, Mimi has worked at "Dot Com. Vision Communications. Century Design" (Hernandez, *Singkil* 56), yet she is unhappy. To her boyfriend, Chase, she says, "Life is not as easy for me as it is for you. Look at you. . . . You are one big fucking smile. All the time. You are a ball of positive energy. And I'm just a black hole. There's nothing inside me. I can't feel anything. And if I can't feel anything, what can I say?" (57). Mimi's inability to put her feelings into words is characteristic of someone who has had a strong affective experience. Brian Massumi argues that unlike emotion—which is "qualified intensity, the conventional, consensual point of insertion of intensity into semantically and semiotically formed progressions, into narrativizable action-reaction circuits, into function and meaning"—affect is not "ownable or recognizable" (28). Although Mimi *says* that she cannot feel anything, she does, in fact, feel something, but it is something that exceeds linguistic representation. Her inability to articulate her feelings could result from a combination of disappointment, threat, or rejection from past experiences. Ahmed explains that "the perception of others as 'causing' an emotional response is not simply my perception, but involves a form of 'contact' between myself and others, which is shaped by longer histories of contact. . . . The intercorporeality of perception depends on histories of reading that come, as it were, 'before' an encounter between subject and another takes place" ("Collective" 31). Upon further questioning, Mimi admits to Chase: "I don't want to tell you that I'm not happy! I don't want to tell you that I cry in the shower! I don't want to tell you that I hate my mother! (*pause*) I don't have anything to say" (Hernandez, *Singkil* 58).

Mimi, we find out through the course of the play, has felt unloved and unwanted by her mother since childhood. There is a history of lack of bonding and communication that has helped shape her affective response to the past and to her mother. Mother-daughter relations have been tense. When Norma, her mother's friend, arrives from the Philippines after the mother's funeral, she tells Mimi that her mother "was very proud of her home country" (21). Mimi replies, "she didn't talk about it much," and comments that she "has never heard about" Norma until then (21). Norma and Mimi's mother used to dance together, but Mimi "didn't know much about [her] mom's years as a dancer" (7). Through several flashbacks, we discover the reasons for this estrangement. In a scene set in 1975, we discover that Maria has ambivalent feelings about motherhood. Just as she is about to give birth to baby Mimi, she says, "I see Nestor about to ceremoniously cut the umbilical cord. I think, 'No! Please don't. Please don't unleash her. Please don't let her . . .'" (31). After giving birth, she feels as if she has fallen into a mother trap: "She wakes, I feed her. I put her to sleep. She wakes, I feed her. I put her to sleep. She wakes, I feed her. I put her to sleep. . . . Stop crying! Oh God, why won't she stop? You want to kill me. My baby wants to kill me. Please stop crying. Please stop crying. Please. Please. Please!" (31). There are signs that Maria is suffering from postpartum depression when she says, "I smile. I notice everyone watching me. They know something is wrong. They keep on asking me if they can help, but the answer is always the same. I don't know. I don't know. If I knew, I would have done it myself. I can't shake this feeling. I can't stop sinking lower into this grey cloud" (31). However, the problem lies deeper.

In her pioneering book *Of Woman Born: Motherhood as Experience and Institution*, second-wave feminist Adrienne Rich writes about the "anger and tenderness" she felt toward her children. She did not fit easily into the identity of a "natural" mother: "I was haunted by the stereotype of the mother whose love is 'unconditional'; and by the visual and literary images of motherhood as a single-minded identity. If I knew parts of myself existed that would never cohere to those images, weren't those parts then abnormal, monstrous?" (22–23). She is unable to reconcile the ideology of motherhood, what she calls the "institution of motherhood," with her own experience and notes that the institution creates "the prescriptions and the conditions in which choices are made or blocked" (42). Rich argues, "certainly the mother serves the interests of patriarchy: she exemplifies in one person religion, social conscience, and nationalism. Institutional motherhood revives and renews all other institutions" (45). Feminist Marxists would call motherhood a kind of ideology or a state apparatus. In poststructuralist terms, Judith Butler discusses the ways in which bodies are "alternately sustained and threatened through modes of address" (*Undoing* 5). She explains, "To understand this, one must imagine an impossible scene, that of a body that has not yet been given social definition, a body, that is, strictly speaking, not accessible to us, that nevertheless becomes accessible on the occasion of an address, a call, an interpellation that does not 'discover' this body, but constitutes it fundamentally" (5).

For Maria, the call or address of mother is antithetical to her earlier life as a principal dancer. She chose to marry Nestor, Mimi's father, and follow him to Canada because she was pregnant before their marriage (Hernandez, *Singkil* 80). The decision was not without difficulty because at the time, both she and her friend Norma were in love with Nestor. Flashbacks of Maria with another man suggest that the marriage was not entirely happy and that she sought refuge from her loneliness and unhappiness through an extramarital affair. For his part, Nestor regrets not having expressed his love for his wife more openly and assertively. For him, the past is also full of emotion, disillusion, and shame, which have affected his masculinity and confidence. There are issues with his work life in addition to his domestic life. Another flashback shows a scene in the 1970s when the CN Tower is being constructed in Toronto. Initially, it seems as if Nestor is proud to be part of building the structure. He says, "The CN Tower is the way of the future . . . the tallest freestanding tower in the world . . . and I will be part of creating it" (36). However, he reveals that he has only a menial job, "pressing buttons and hammering nails" on site. He says, "I never have the courage to tell anyone I graduated from the University of Santo Tomas, College of Architecture" (36–37). Nestor is an immigrant who suffers from underemployment and a lack of recognition of his credentials from Asia. Like Mimi's, his relation to the past exceeds verbal representation. For both of Mimi's parents, then, immigration to Canada has required compromises and reconciliation between expectations, desires, and the practical needs of the everyday. They both live with a sense of the lives they could have led, the careers they could have had, had history been different.

In the 2007 Toronto staging of the play, a woven mat made of rattan and straw covered the raised stage, which concealed some compartments. Mimi found items from the past under the stage, such as the box containing her mother's dance headpiece. Symbolically, the past is buried underneath and needs uncovering. Mimi has not been able to discuss events in her past, such as her mother's infidelity, with anyone. Only after her mother's death does she discover that her father knew about her mother's affair. Nestor tells her, "All those years, I did it for you. I stayed for you. . . . You wonder why I stuck around when I knew what was going on, when I could smell the scent of cigarettes and cologne on her neck? You would understand if you could look into the eyes of your child and see that she needs you" (73). She discovers that her parents' marriage was a failure, a sham for her sake. While this revelation does not necessarily smooth their relationship, it puts father and daughter on a path of reconciliation and healing, as they both start to understand how their silence and refusal to acknowledge their own pain have isolated them.

First, Mimi goes to her mother's grave to ask her spirit for forgiveness and to tell her the things she neglected to say when Maria was alive. Then, she tells Chase that she loves him and thanks him for being there for her. This effort is important because it is an attempt to not replicate the relationship her mother and father had, which was one based on secrecy and mistrust. An earlier scene suggested that Chase could be turning to another woman while Mimi struggles with her feelings. Mimi stops herself from becoming like her mother, prevent-ing a repetition of the triangular relationship by opening up to her boyfriend instead of not communicating with him about her fears. She saves herself from being burdened by history and by her past. In the larger context of Asian North American literature, Mimi's ability to negotiate with her past is important because it shows that second-generation young adults can resist the immigrant generation's fatalism without completely rejecting their ethnicity.

Resolution comes in the play through art and ethnic heritage. Mimi is helped by her mother's friend Norma, who tells her that Maria danced the singkil while pregnant with Mimi, and that Mimi has been "dancing the singkil" her entire life (82). Norma says:

> Most people think it's about a Muslim princess who gets caught in the middle of an earthquake and her betrothed prince saves her. That's the story your mom knew. Here, alone in Canada. Making it through hard times, waiting. Waiting to be happy. When everything to make her happy was right in front of her ... Your mom was wrong. I was wrong. I was waiting, too. There is no prince. That's just the theatrical version. The prince was added for drama. The real story is of a princess that saves herself. (82)

Norma presents Mimi with an up-to-date and feminist revision of the legend depicted in the singkil, putting the onus on Mimi to take responsibility for her own life and stop being angry with other people.

Hernandez's choice of the singkil dance is significant and suggestive. *Singkil* is the "Maranao word for getting a leg or foot entangled in an object, where a solo female performer dances in and out of criss-crossed bamboo poles, keeping time to a hypnotic rhythm, all the while waving her fans gracefully" (2). Traditionally, it is a dance performed by a woman of royal blood to advertise to would-be suitors for her future marriage. "Legend has it that singkil originated from the day the *diwatas* (some form of nymph or fairy) played a joke on Princess Gandingan as she was taking a walk in the woods. The *diwatas* caused an earthquake that made the trees tremble and the rocks to roll and knock against each other. [Undaunted], Princess Gandingan skipped nimbly from place to place and no tree or rock ever touched her tiny feet" (Aquino). The dance entails skill and grace on the performer's part. "The dance has no definite number of steps or figures. Even the arm movements are improvised and executed according to the mood and skill of the dancers" (Aquino). Even for contemporary Filipinos, the singkil dance is formal and somewhat exotic. The dance is culturally specific, but the message of self-reliance has a wide appeal.

The play's final scene features Mimi wearing her mother's *Sari Manok* dance costume and preparing to dance. The ending is significant because it suggests that Mimi is embracing rather than rejecting the father, the mother, and the motherland. In spite of the mother's inability to bond with her daughter, Mimi is able to go beyond her raw emotions and find a way to connect with her mother. The singkil dance requires concentration, discipline, and self-confidence. As a symbol of Mimi's future, the dance suggests that there are obstacles and problems to overcome in life's journey but that it is possible to step over these nimbly and with grace if she concentrates and keeps looking forward. Second-generation immigrants like Mimi do not have to repeat their parents' mistakes but can harness their energy, passion, creativity, and intelligence to go forward. The play demonstrates that second-generation children want more out of life than their immigrant parents did. As we have seen, Mimi is not content with only economic successes, as immigrants of the 1960s and 1970s would have been. Her various dot-com jobs have left her feeling empty, and she wishes for affective pleasure from her life. She wants work to be more than a job and her relationship to be more than an outwardly happy conventional marriage. For second-generation immigrants, survival, assimilation, and belonging are not enough; the search for happiness is also important. They are not afraid to desire and wish for what their parents were promised. Instead of being burdened by their past, they use it selectively and are bold enough to rewrite folktales and myths, if necessary. The path ahead is not rosy or laid out for Mimi. She will have to rely on her own skills and wits to shape her future. But she is on her way to becoming her own kind of princess, as her mother would have been.

Failure in Public in *Out of the Blue*

Even though Chinese Canadians have been in the country for over 150 years, only a handful of Chinese Canadians have become media celebrities and have achieved national recognition. With the exception of the Olympic silver medalist figure skater Patrick Chan 陳偉群, the Canadians of Chinese origin we recognize in the media are mostly women: Adrienne Clarkson 伍冰枝, broadcaster and journalist of thirty years, who was Canada's twenty-sixth governor general from 1999 to 2005; Vivienne Poy 利德蕙, businesswoman, chancellor of the University of Toronto (2003–2006), and first Canadian senator of Asian ancestry (1998–2012); and Jan Wong 黃明珍, journalist, Beijing correspondent (1988–1994), and professor. These women's extraordinary lives demonstrate the possibilities of the Canadian immigrant dream (Canada's equivalent of the American dream), where immigrants start out in difficult political and economic circumstances but become successful models and citizens through hard work and perseverance.

As discussed in the introduction, in the United States, where there is a more explicit discourse on race, Asians have been held up as the "model minority" since the late 1960s, used as examples against blacks and Latinos who do not fare as well in schools or in professional accomplishments. The much-quoted article published in the *U.S. News and World Report* in December 1966 lauded "Chinese Americans for their remarkable achievements and praised Chinatowns as bastions of peace and prosperity" (Osajima). As Keith Osajima notes, "the accomplishments of less than one-million Asian Americans emerged as a model for how all minority groups could 'make it' in society" (216–17). These stereotypes about Asians and the myth of the model minority created unreasonable expectations for Asians that were and are very difficult to meet. Although Canadians do not publicly use the term *model minority*, stereotypes of Asians persist in Canadian popular culture and discourse. Asians are supposed to excel in certain areas, namely mathematics, computers, engineering, and playing the violin, and they are viewed as sheltered nerds and geeks who have little or no social life because they do nothing but study. Studies show that Asian Americans suffer from higher rates of stress, depression, mental illness, and suicide attempts than other races (NAWHO). Though "Asian Fail" Tumblr blogs feature jokes about Asians, usually posted by Asians who laugh at their own foolish mistakes and quirky characteristics, there are serious social, psychic, and physical consequences for Asian North Americans who see themselves as failures. Jan Wong's story is about the depression that ensues from living a life in the public eye. What happens to one's identity when one fails at doing the work at which one is supposed to be good?

FIGURE 4. One night stand meme

Wong's book about her experience with work-related stress and depression can be read partly as an illustration of an extended "Asian Fail," though in a different way from the funny examples on the Tumblr blog. Even though it was not meant to outline the many ways one can fail to live up to being a typical or stereotypical "Asian," it does do that in several places. The self-published memoir gives an account of the events that led to her being fired from the *Globe and Mail*, her subsequent depression, and her struggle to come to terms with her illness. She performs multiple acts of cultural translation, including educating the general public about depression and mental illness, writing an autoethnographic account of what it means to belong to a Chinese diasporic community, and explaining her failure as an Asian Canadian woman. Eva Karpinski notes of translation theory: "Taking the cultural turn, translation has become reconceived as part of the process of cultural representation and interchange, an interactive textual practice of transcoding and constructing meanings and selves cross-culturally" (11). My reading examines the ways in which Wong performs acts of translation across different divides—racial and ethnic, gender, public and private—as she seeks in her memoir to find a subjectivity other than that of a journalist.

While covering the news about the 2006 Dawson College shootings in Montreal, Jan Wong thought she had found a brilliant thread connecting three school shootings in Quebec. For Wong, the fact that the gunman, Kimveer Gill, was the son of immigrants from India was significant and led her to remember that "another campus shooting in Montreal had also involved an immigrant, a Russian named Valery Fabrikant, who had killed four colleagues at Concordia University" (Jan Wong 31). In the "bloodiest campus shooting, Marc Lépine had murdered fourteen women at Ecole Polytechnique" (31). After some quick research, Wong discovered that Lépine was born Gamil Gharbi and was the son of a Muslim businessman from Algeria. Wong then made the leap from immigrant children to the alienating effect of the linguistic struggle in Quebec, suggesting that the perpetrator in all three cases "was not *pure laine*, the argot for a 'pure' francophone," and therefore must have felt alienated in Quebec (31). In one paragraph, she had, in essence, practiced a kind of ethnic profiling of second-generation immigrants and then also implied that Quebec is a racist society: "Elsewhere, to talk of racial 'purity' is repugnant. Not in Quebec" (31). Without solid proof, she argued that all three killers "had been marginalized, in a society that valued *pure laine*" (32).

Used to being a provocateur, Wong did not expect the virulence of the hate e-mails she received subsequent to this story in the *Globe and Mail*. She received personal insults—"stupid cunt," "pathetic," "perverted," "racist pig," etc.—as well as death threats. Initially, she was nonplussed, thinking that the backlash might even make a good story. But then her family was attacked: some people called for a boycott of her family's restaurant, her children were getting racist taunts, and she was caricatured in *Le Devoir*. Expecting the support of her editors at the *Globe and Mail*, she felt betrayed when they distanced themselves and the paper from her. It was at this time that her breakdown began. Ordered not to talk to the media, she felt "herself disintegrating" (44). When she found herself unable to write, the paper's management fired her, not believing that she was ill.

Wong's book *Out of the Blue* chronicles the depression and recovery that took about five years. It is a cross between a memoir, an apology or defense of her life, a research essay about depression, and an exposé of management at the *Globe and Mail*, the big and "mean" corporation. Of all these genres, the essay/memoir about depression is the most successful. As a defense and a memoir of a Chinese Canadian female journalist, it is awkward and at times even off-putting, possibly because, as reviewer Anne Kingston notes, "only one version of events is presented," and Wong does have a "tendency to see the world in black-and-white terms of betrayer and betrayed." Sidonie Smith and Julia Watson have noted the difficulty of writing about breakdowns: "The life narrator describing a breakdown from an asserted position of recovery is always suspect. How can memoirists authorize themselves as postbreakdown writers?" (145). Like other stories of breakdown, Wong's narrative "foregrounds challenges to telling a credible story. . . . She both produces and undermines the truth effect of her narrative, marking the boundary between the fabulated and the documented as unstable" (146). Normally, there is not enough drama in one's everyday struggles with depression to keep readers' attention riveted, but because Jan Wong had established herself as a media personality through her famous "Lunch With" column (1996–2002) and her position as the *Globe and Mail*'s China correspondent from 1988 to 1994, she had a following. Wong's *Out of the Blue* hit the *Toronto Star*'s best-seller list at the end of May 2012, within a month after it appeared—a very rare feat for a self-published book. The only precedents were David Chilton's *The Wealthy Barber* (1989) and Terry Fallis's *The Best Laid Plans* (2008).

The book's success may have had something to do with Wong's tenacity. What brought her to the public eye also brought her down because she had become such a public figure and was widely read. The backlash from her ill-conceived statements about the school shootings came from all over the country. A few days after her article about the three killers being marginalized came out, she "received hundreds of hate emails" (Jan Wong 33), and then, as the

Globe and Mail published some of these letters, the number swelled to thousands. Wong described it as a kind of "internet stoning" and compared it to being "pilloried in medieval stocks" (34). It was the first time, Wong said, that she was attacked for her race, and she fell apart: "I went from being a reporter who could pull off a three-thousand-word feature in one day to someone who could no longer write at all" (32). Ironically, like many people who are driven and ambitious in their profession, Wong became a victim of her own success and the neoliberal belief in hard work. She writes, "I work, therefore I am. Without my job, I didn't know who I was. . . . Our culture holds that work is good. Therefore, not working makes us feel guilty" (55). When she found herself unable to write, she lost her sense of self; in retrospect, she realizes that her "deep emotional investment" in her work had set her up for a "major depressive episode" (55). In her book *Depression*, Ann Cvetkovich argues that "depression, or alternative accounts of what gets called depression, is . . . a way to describe neoliberalism and globalization, or the current state of political economy, in affective terms. . . . Depression can be seen as a category that manages and medicalizes the affects associated with keeping up with corporate culture and the market economy, or with being completely neglected by it" (11–12).

What Cvetkovich contends in her book is that depression is a "cultural and social phenomenon rather than a medical disease" (1). She writes, "What gets called depression in the domestic sphere is one affective register of . . . social problems and one that often keeps people silent, weary and too numb to really notice the sources of their unhappiness" (12). Whether or not we are conscious of them, "everyday life produces feelings of despair and anxiety, sometimes extreme, sometimes throbbing along at a low level, and hence barely discernible" (14). Instead of just finding the right drugs for people to take, Cvetkovich is interested in "forms of flexibility or creativity," including "different ways of being able to move: to solve problems, have ideas, be joyful about the present, make things" (21). She studies texts about depression that "combine memoir and critical analysis" and ones that use the memoir form "other than that of the conventional medical case history or sensational confession, including its value as research report, speculative fiction, and creative articulation of public feelings" (141). Wong's memoir is one example of a work that combines life-writing with research. Even though Wong's style is informal and chatty, she tries to weave her findings about depression into her narrative, and her lengthy bibliography at the end of the memoir suggests that she has read several studies about the condition. What she does, in effect, is translate her research on mental illness and depression into accessible language and into life-writing.

Wong analyzes her depression, describing its various stages, linking her case to other examples, and providing a historical account of the illness. Early on, she notes, "Memory is the first casualty of depression. I forgot appointments. When I remembered them, I could no longer calculate when I had to leave the house in order to arrive at my destination on time. It was as if my brain had shut down" (Jan Wong 77). She compares herself to William Styron, who also went through all the "classic symptoms: initial denial, confusion, memory lapses, self-loathing, and failure of mental focus" (77). Even though she was bursting into tears at the doctor's office and then crying all the way home on the subway, she was in denial at first. But she uses her reading of other people's experiences and her research into the history of melancholia to understand her situation: "Depression is not a benign illness. It is a form of madness. I lost my rationality, sense of reality, proportionality. Everything happened, quite literally, in my head" (81–82). Her itemizing of the "symptoms of depression: depressed mood, diminished interest or pleasure in normal daily activities, loss of appetite, inability to sleep, psychomotor retardation, fatigue, feelings of worthlessness, diminished ability to think or concentrate, recurrent thoughts of death" (82) enables her to assess her own condition and compare herself with others diagnosed with clinical depression.

Another way she empowers herself is through feminist politics. Her work-place depression triggers a memory of a previous time when she also felt depressed, albeit for a short time. In 1990, after the birth of her son Ben, she felt blue and "burst into tears for no apparent reason" (102). Although this feeling disappeared a few weeks later, she reflects, in retrospect, that it was probably "low-grade postpartum depression," which she had not acknowledged at the time (102). She links that brief experience to her present situation and comments, "We are twice as likely as men to suffer from depression, even though men are four times as likely to commit suicide" (103). She notes that there are various theories about why women are so susceptible, including women's hormones and biochemistry; the way women tend to "ruminate" and "process their feelings by thinking and thinking and thinking"; and the fact that in a male-dominated world, women "are more likely than men to be poor, disenfranchised, uneducated, unemployed or fired, . . . more likely to be sexually abused" (103). Her own experience with depression leads her to think of these larger social issues and conventions that cause more depression in women than in men. She also remembers and retrospectively understands what her mother went through during her last years of life after suffering from a stroke and then cancer. Like her mother, Wong "lost weight steadily" because her digestive system had shut down (109). It was only then that she understood how "stress impacts metabolism" (108). Her narration of these incidents, coupled with research, produces an account of depression that is critical and political, as she translates medical research for a popular audience.

Throughout her depression, Wong does not just passively take the drugs her doctor prescribes; she also tries different kinds of therapies, including music, travel, and shopping. Her friends and extended family support her in these endeavours. Her sixteen-year-old son, who did not like classical concerts himself, takes her to hear the Toronto Symphony Orchestra, where she finds, "To my surprise, the doleful descending passages felt like a balm. To my further surprise, research has found that misery does love company, that melancholy songs comfort sad people by signaling that they are not alone" (65). Invited by the president of the North Toronto Community Band to join the band, she takes up her flute again and finds pleasure in playing "a repertoire of marches, jazz, big band, Disney medleys, soft rock, and . . . classical music" (119). When her doctor encourages her to get out of town, she travels to her friend's cottage, to New York, to Paris, and, with her son's hockey team, to Finland and Sweden. She writes, "Although the sadness stayed with me, travel did transport me away from the rancid crust of everyday misery. . . . Travel means being distracted by new details, new things, new logistics" (73).

Part of her healing process also includes shopping: "It seemed a sociable but safe way to be around other people without the obligation of real intimacy" (196). She writes, "When I had ten minutes available before a doctor's appointment, I bought crystal candlesticks. In the spare five minutes before meeting friends at the theater, I dashed into Payless Shoes and bought a cheap pair of strappy black sandals. On my way to the Royal Ontario Museum, I ducked into Talbots and emerged with a pair of black trousers to add to my collection of seventeen other pairs of black trousers" (196). To explain her shopaholic tendencies, she alludes to a literary work as well as a biochemical theory: "One hundred and fifty years ago, Flaubert understood the emotional tug of shopping. In *Madame Bovary*, his bored heroine is trapped in a loveless marriage to a dull, provincial doctor and frantically tries to shop her way to happiness—with tragic consequences. Each time *I* bought something, even a stupid hockey T-shirt, I felt inexplicably happy" (197). According to her psychiatrist, "Shopping activates the brain's reward center, releasing a gush of dopamine, the same happy chemical triggered by gambling, drug use and other addictive behaviors" (197). Her own theory is that shopping is linked to the hunter-gatherer instinct, and that gathering, even of shoes, can be "as exciting as hunting" (198).

This therapy, however, is available only to those who can afford it. One of the most important lessons in her book is how having money provides one with a cushion during clinical depression. In an interview with *CBC News*, Wong said, "For people who don't have that economic independence, it's crushing. That's why this book is so important. I want employers and employees and HR professionals to understand. For companies, you're just going to have to spend more money if you fight it. It's going to end up costing you more. Understand that when your employees are sick, they are sick" (Clibbon). At points like this, it becomes hard to sympathize with Wong. Her seemingly powerful advocacy for workers is diminished by her personal habits. When she talks about shopping for prints, or for fur coats on sale for seven thousand dollars, and signing up for a nineteen-hundred-dollar refinishing of her dining-room table (196–97), albeit during her depression, can we still relate to her as Chinese Canadian? Or perhaps the larger question this narrative raises is, How can the existing politics of Asian Canadian or Chinese Canadian studies still be predicated on the myth of the hard-working, oppressed immigrant? It is hard to claim group solidarity with someone who behaves so impulsively and irresponsibly, even in illness.

Although the Asian Canadian community is heterogeneous, certain cultural stereotypes about Chinese Canadians persist, such as the Confucianist belief in filial piety, emphasis on education and academic achievement, strong family values, and the importance of saving and taking care of parents. In her memoir, Wong admits that the ways she has treated her sister, her parents, and her husband have not been very considerate. In the realm of traditional Confucian qualities, Wong seems a good example of "Asian Fail."

In her account, Jan Wong talks about how she left her sister, Gigi, to cover all their shared duties toward their parents. She notes that she and Gigi "have always been very different. I left home at eighteen and didn't look back. Gigi never severed ties with our parents. After her marriage ended, she moved back into our parents' home with her two toddlers. . . . I am forever grateful that Gigi took care of our parents as they aged. She accompanied them to every doctor's appointment. . . . the entire burden of care fell on my sister. She kept vigil at each operation" (27). Wong says she tried to help, but she "didn't stick around. . . . I lived in Toronto and I had to get back to work. . . . I loved my mother but I didn't feel I could take time off work" (27). Jan was not there when Gigi had to take their mother off life support, and Gigi was so angry that she severed her relationship with Jan for several years. Similarly, Jan neglects her husband, Norman:

> I had never paid much attention to Norman's work. He is a systems engineer. Although he had steadfastly supported my career, following me from Beijing to New York to Montreal to Boston to Toronto and back to Beijing again, I had scarcely reciprocated. In fact, whenever I had insomnia, my solution was

to nudge him awake and ask about his doctoral thesis. He would become *animated*, well, not quite animated, but he would start talking at length about parallel programming languages and the semantics of shared variables. As he droned on, I would fall deeply asleep, leaving *him* wide-awake. (37)

She says of her selfish behavior, "I justified this spousal abuse as feminism" (37), linking her single-minded concentration on her career to the influence of feminists of the 1960s.

How has our society come to a point where the pressures to succeed in a career have made it impossible for us to pay attention to our affective ties? Though she does not come out and say it, Wong's success as a journalist has been achieved at the expense of her familial life. Only during her depression does she recognize that over the years, she has put her own needs before the needs of family members—her mother, her husband, even her children. She has become an example not only of an "Asian Fail" (by not acting according to Confucian ideals of self-sacrifice and female subservience) but also of a corporate workaholic. One way of reading her failure to live up to our expectations of "Chineseness" is to see her as the overachiever immigrant: she has been so thoroughly engrossed with reaching the top that she has not been able to fulfill other responsibilities or enjoy other aspects of her life.

In one sense, the depression has been good for her, as it has forced her to look closely at herself and her life. She concludes her memoir on a positive note:

> Today we live in a culture where we define ourselves almost solely by what *we do*. I finally understand how emotionally vulnerable that makes us, especially during economic crises when so many people lose their jobs. As Socrates told the Athenians at his trial for heresy, "the unexamined life is not worth living." I had been living the unexamined life. I mistook the buoyant surface of success for happiness. And then an amazingly quick series of events stripped everything away. I was forced to learn about who I am and what really matters. That is the gift of depression: it makes you withdraw and gives you time for reflection. . . . People who emerge from depression often find a heightened awareness of the beauty of everyday existence. To appreciate a brilliantly sunny day, there must also be a night. I now derive joy from things I had never noticed before, had no time for, when I was racing to meet deadlines. (251)

Being Asian, she has translated her failure into a best-seller in spite of the odds against her.

CHAPTER 6

Gender, Post-9/11, and Ugly Feelings

Chapter 5 looked at work-related depression and failure, and the ways in which professional labor in today's corporate world shapes our contemporary subjectivities. When their professional lives do not work out as planned, the women in the works examined in that chapter suffer from psychic and emotional consequences, which they eventually resolve in part through artistic endeavours. Writing a book of memoirs or dancing becomes a way of breaking the mental impasse and overcoming the feeling of failure. Chapter 3 explored the haunting effects of war and displacement on immigrants, second-generation Asian North Americans, and refugees. In this chapter, I look at two texts that use humor and irony to deal with broken dreams and with ugly feelings caused by the inability perform the dominant culture's expectations of race and gender. The protagonists in Alex Gilvarry's postmodern novel *From the Memoirs of a Non-Enemy Combatant* and in Keshni Kashyap and Mari Araki's *Tina's Mouth: An Existential Comic Diary* struggle to dissolve rigid categories of masculinity, femininity, and race. They both want to lead the lives of ordinary Americans but instead are forced to work through cultural expectations generated by their brown bodies, answering to the hopes of their families and friends and to the fantasies created by literature, film, and media. Gilvarry's novel is much darker than Kashyap and Araki's, but both stories exemplify twenty-first-century failures.

Masculinity, Race, and the Post-9/11 Narrative in
From the Memoirs of a Non-Enemy Combatant

In his witty and humorous first novel, disguised as "memoirs," Alex Gilvarry pushes at numerous boundaries: of genre, gender, and ethnonology/race. The book is about an immigrant from the Philippines who comes to the United States with the quintessential American dream, but instead of following the usual pattern of immigration, acculturation, and settlement, the novel turns into a failed-immigrant narrative and a critique of the American justice system and democracy. At one level, the book is a postmodern pastiche; it partakes of postmodern parodic self-reflexivity and irony and is a satire of the New York fashion industry. However, through a series of unfortunate coincidences that happen to the narrator, the book takes on a darker tone and becomes a post-9/11 novel, even though the narrator attempts to maintain a lighthearted attitude throughout his memoirs. As the Filipino protagonist is misidentified as a Middle Eastern terrorist, the work reflects concerns that South Asian and Arab Americans faced in the years following 2001, expanding the boundaries of what we call Asian American to forge connections between South Asian, Middle Eastern, and Southeast Asian ethnic groups.

The first half of this chapter examines the narrative techniques—intertexuality, extratextuality, and use of irony—in *Memoirs of a Non-Enemy Combatant*. I read the novel as a quirky, original, and darkly comic response to 9/11. After 2001, a number of post-9/11 novels sprang up; with one or two exceptions, they tend to be set in various locations in Manhattan and depict lives of everyday Americans before and after the fall of the World Trade Center. Examples include Jonathan Safran Foer's *Extremely Loud and Incredibly Close* (2005), Don DeLillo's *Falling Man* (2007), Claire Messud's *The Emperor's Children* (2006), and Joseph O'Neill's *Netherland* (2008). Other novels, not set in New York, have been influenced by the "War on Terror," such as Ian McEwan's *Saturday* (2005), Mohsin Hamid's *The Reluctant Fundamentalist* (2007), and Laila Halaby's *Once in a Promised Land* (2007). One blogger from the *Daily Beast* notes that "the great 9/11 novel . . . doesn't want to be spotted" because "Sept. 11 is a black hole that can't be approached directly" (So). Instead, he writes, the novels deal with 9/11 in "oblique ways" (So).

Domestic Space as Retreat after 9/11

Critic Magali Michael argues that a novel such as Don DeLillo's *Falling Man* "depicts a world in which the events of 9/11 so fully invalidate any notion of the self as whole, unified, powerful or as having any control or agency that the novel and its characters' task becomes one of finding alternative forms of order and stability as temporary grounds from which to salvage the shards of humanity and self to which they hang precariously" (74). She points out that DeLillo's novel counters "the reactionary bent of the dominant narratives created and disseminated by the media and the Bush administration following 9/11, which overtly reasserted and championed traditional notions of heroic, militarized masculinity that privilege physical strength and the power accorded by such strength" (73–74). She writes, "DeLillo's novel addresses and attempts to move past the trauma triggered by the recognition that neither the individual nor the nation is impregnable or invincible by creating a *counter-narrative*... using and molding for its own purposes a version of the domestic novel—a narrative form *not* usually associated with masculinity" (74).

Amy Kaplan, in her essay "Manifest Domesticity," "links the familial household to the nation" and "imagines both in opposition to everything outside the geographic and conceptual border of home" (581) so that "men and women become national allies against the alien" (582). Magali Michael writes,

> the novel creates a narrative in which the communal ties of family accentu-
> ated by an ethics of care, the familiar physical spaces that create a conception
> of home, and the rituals of daily bodily existence provide a kind of psycho-
> logical grounding for the shattered self and a means of beginning to recover
> a sense of shared humanity in the face of inhumanity....
> ... Rituals entail sets of repeated culturally constructed and validated or-
> dered actions or tasks that create a sense of soothing predictability as well
> as of agency for the person performing the rituals and, in most cultures, is
> often associated with the domestic sphere even though, in practice, rituals
> structure the public as well as domestic spheres of cultures. (75–76, 79)

In Alex Gilvarry's *Memoirs of a Non-Enemy Combatant*, there is no domestic stability, comfortable ritual, or ordered set of actions for the protagonist, who claims he was "born again" when he arrived in America: "propelled through the duct of JFK International, out the rotating doors, *push, push*, dripping a post–U.S. Customs sweat down my back, and slithering out on my feet to a curb in Queens, *breathe*. Then into a yellow cab, thrown to the masses" (3). Boyet Hernandez dates one or two women, but he is not married, and he lives as an itinerant in America. He does not manage to find a home or family but is "thrown to the masses" after his American rebirth. First, he stays in an apart-ment owned by a model friend, where he discovers that he is to share the bed (platonically) with another model, Olya. Then he finds a "tiny studio apartment in Bushwick, Brooklyn" that was a "kind of exile" for "anyone who worked in fashion" (28). More than a year after he arrived in New York, his living quarters are "marked by a mere mattress on the floor and a few bar stools" because he hasn't yet "found much time to furnish" (135). When he goes shopping with his then girlfriend Michelle at the Swedish furniture warehouse one day, Boyet feels as if the "living rooms and bedrooms and bathrooms of Swedish modernity" are unreal, like "a stage," and that they are "walking through sets like actors in one giant play, pretending" (136). Boyet's sense of alienation from scenes of domesticity suggests that he is reluctant or unable to participate in one of the social scripts needed for happiness in contemporary America, that of living within the heterosexual family unit. He feels that Michelle and he are only "pretend lovers" (136) and that he is never embraced by his adopted country even though he asserts, "I love America" (3). Unlike other post-9/11 novels, *Memoirs* does not find a comfortable solution from the terrorist events of 9/11 through the home. Instead, Boyet is thrown into "No Man's Land" (the Guántanamo Bay detention camp) in 2006, just after he has broken into the fashion industry, into "Bryant Park after six seasons in New York" (19).

The structure of *Memoirs of a Non-Enemy Combatant* juxtaposes chapters recounting Boyet's arrival as an immigrant with chapters about his detention in the (Guántanamo) cell, "approximately six feet by eight feet," where the "walls are steel mesh" and where the bed "is a metal plank affixed to one side" (20). This alternating narrative structure provides a Kafkaesque, nightmarish atmosphere to the novel. Frederick R. Karl, Kafka's biographer, explains, "What's Kafkaesque . . . is when you enter a surreal world in which all your control patterns, all your plans, the whole way in which you have configured your own behavior, begins to fall to pieces, when you find yourself against a force that does not lend itself to the way you perceive the world" (qtd. in Edwards). Gilvarry's novel, though darkly humorous, presents this kind of surreal world of misrecognition and misidentification. Without warning, Boyet goes from being a high-fashion designer to being a terrorist; his climb to financial and social success is abruptly halted.

Middle Eastern, South Asian, Southeast Asian, and Race

Joshua Takano Chambers-Letson draws parallels between the detention of Japanese Americans during World War II and the "profiling and detention of brown America" (151). He writes, "The regime of detention, surveillance, and imprisonment that insinuates itself increasingly into the lives of racialized subjects continues to produce Asian immigrants and Asian American subjects as always already 'illegal'" (151). Boyet is detained and transported to No Man's Land because of his friendship with Ahmed Qureshi, a Pakistani who "was arrested for selling bomb-making materials" (Gilvarry 37) in 2006. Ahmed claimed to have come from Canada, and Boyet "was able to overlook his lies no matter how blatant" because Ahmed offered him twenty-five hundred dollars to design two suits for him (35). Though Boyet is somewhat suspicious when he sees "large wooden crates marked FRAGILE" in Ahmed's apartment, he wants Ahmed's business too much to pay attention to those suspicions. Later, he realizes that the "U.S. Department of Defense does not take these things lightly. That an innocent conversation on origins could be used as sufficient evidence to be detained by the Department of Homeland Security, or as conclusive evidence of conspiring by DoD" (55).

Boyet notices early on that as a Filipino American, he shares similar characteristics with a Pakistani. When he first meets Ahmed, he notices that "he was a foreigner, too. Our skin color was the same deep sienna" (29). At another point, when Boyet is walking around Forty-Second Street, he sees a South Asian man who resembles him, begging passersby to take menus from him. Boyet notes, "Our resemblance was remarkable. Like me he was five foot one, nearly a foot below the average New Yorker. He seemed to share my same build. . . . His eyebrows were overgrown and had formed a prominent unibrow, whereas I plucked mine daily. . . . His hands were just like mine" (15). The similarity in their appearance creates an epiphanic moment for Boyet, who realizes that the same city that gives so much opportunity to immigrants could "reduce a virile young man to dressing up as a menu on Forty-second Street, pleading, 'Take one, take one, please, take one'" (16). He concludes early on that "dreams could be realized on these streets" but that "mostly, dreams were crushed in this city" (17).

This observation about the similarities in appearance between himself and a South Asian immigrant takes on darker implications when Boyet is thrown into No Man's Land. In his cell, along with the standard-issue blanket, towel, exercise mat/mattress, toothbrush, water bottle, and flip-flops, he receives "religious paraphernalia" consisting of "one standard-issue Qur'an . . . one foam prayer rug, one white skullcap, one plastic vial of oil (patchouli)" (20). Boyet tries to tell the jailers that "these items are completely useless" because he is "no Muslim" but was "baptized a Catholic" (20), but to no avail. As the tailor of a man charged with selling bomb-making materials, Boyet becomes misidentified and categorized into what Inderpal Grewal calls a "collective subject described as

'Middle Eastern' or Muslim" (535) man. The problem of racial misrecognition is not new to Filipino Americans; they have been invisible and underrepresented in mainstream U.S. popular culture (see Ty, *Politics* 28; Ponce 186–205). But in this novel, a Filipino American is misrecognized not as a Latino or Chinese person but as a Muslim Middle Easterner. Grewal notes that American multiculturalism, along with concepts such as "hyphenated or mestizo identities," has facilitated the "strategies of self-identification and difference" that challenge the "normative white, male, heterosexual Anglo-American citizen" (538) and has enabled more flexible and changing subject formations. However, emerging after 9/11 were discourses of "risk" and "security," where certain gendered and racialized bodies were categorized as high risk: "The Muslim as terrorist and the racialised figure of the person who 'looks like a Muslim' as a racial figure of the 'terrorist' thus emerge at the present time as part of this visual history within consumer culture of managing and destroying those who are believed to provide the highest risk to the nation" (540). What is ironic and comic, albeit darkly so, about Boyet is that he belongs to the category of "looks like a Muslim" only because of his appearance, because he is brown. However, he hardly fits into the popular culture imagination of the new Oriental, which, as Grewal notes, is "not a categorisation based on language, blood, or continental origins, but one based on facial characteristics of beards, dark eyes, and turbans; on discourses of fanaticism and violence; and on origins in West or South Asia or the Middle East" (547).

Re-emergence of Western Cowboy Masculinity

Michael Kimmel argues that 9/11 was responsible for a major transformation in gender debates. Kimmel notes that "by the turn of the new century, masculinity was on parade everywhere one looked, especially in the media. From the relentlessly and unapologetically sexist *The Man Show* and scores of magazines like *Maxim* and *Details*, to movies in which young children humanize stoic men (including Tom Cruise, John Cusack, and The Rock) into emotionally available—and happier—men, to the more consciously gender-bending TV shows *Boy Meets Boy* and *Queer Eye for the Straight Guy*, masculinity has been paraded before us, consciously and intentionally, as perhaps never before" (4–5). For Kimmel, the concept of masculinity was expanding in the 1990s, and only a few sectors remained mainly male strongholds. On "September 10, 2001, . . . firefighters, police officers, and soldiers represented some of the last remaining resisters of gender equality" (6), but the "events since 9/11 reversed the fortunes of . . . images of masculinity" (6). After September 11, "the rehabilitation of heroic masculinity among firefighters, police, and other rescue workers was immediate" (6). In addition, militarized masculinity of the Bush-Cheney years replaced corporate masculinity, which was reeling from the dot-com bubble (7). "It was tragically ironic that the idealization of military masculinity of the Bush years, coupled with the post-9/11 canonization of firefighters and police, led to the reassertion of traditional gender ideologies—in the very country that was attacked by those who found our gender ideologies too liberal and sought to impose even more traditional policies" (7). Susan Faludi notes, "In the post-9/11 reenactment of the fifties Western, women figured largely as vulnerable maidens. Never mind that the fatalities that day were three-to-one male-to-female and that most of the female office workers at the World Trade Center (like their male counterparts) rescued themselves by walking down the stairs on their own two feet" (6).

Unfortunately, Boyet Hernandez, being a small man of five foot one in "peak physical condition" (Gilvarry 8), does not fit the traditional image of Western masculinity, those strong firefighters and police ready to protect distressed females. Because he is a fashion designer for women and has smooth legs and no beard (55), people ask him frequently if he is homosexual, but he says, "I like women. Blondes" (33). Yet as his financial backer, Ahmed, notices, he is a "man-child" with "hairless arms," a "chest bare like a woman" (55). When Michelle, whom he ends up dating for two years, first meets him, she says, "You're a *straight* fashion designer? That is so ironic" (101). In prison, he is branded as a homosexual, and the other inmates call him a "foggot" (91). Boyet is caught in a no-man's-land of gender identification. Although he is not the image of the newly revived heroic masculinity, neither is he the Oriental with the bearded turban; the fact that he is nevertheless deemed alien and high risk reveals the hysteria of the post-9/11 years, when the "us and them" antiterrorist discourse constructed by Bush and the popular media allowed very little room for masculine subjectivities that did not fit the American notions of gender divisions.

Historiographic Metafiction and Irony

In terms of genre, *Memoirs of a Non-Enemy Combatant* exhibits many characteristics of what Linda Hutcheon calls historiographic metafiction, those "well-known and popular novels which are both intensely self-reflexive and yet paradoxically also lay claim to historical events and personages" (*Poetics* 5). In an interview with the *Economist*, Alex Gilvarry acknowledges that the book is a composite of "real" and fictional characters: "A lot of the designers in the book are real, and they worked because they're larger than life—they're almost fictitious. I used a lot of real detainees because it was important to infuse the book with a certain seriousness. And then there were people like George Bush and Dick Cheney," whom he didn't want to name outright (A.G.). The memoirist and protagonist, Boyet Hernandez, uses epigraphs from fashion designers that are supposed to be profound but sometimes end up trite, funny, or ludicrous. For example, the book's main epigraph is from Coco Chanel: "Since everything is in our heads, we had better not lose them" (Gilvarry [v]). At times, however, the mundane becomes paradoxically philosophical. Describing the way a gown fitted on Ahmed, Boyet notes, "I actually admired the gown's free-flowing elegance. It was airy and had a lot of movement. It somehow covered up the fact that underneath was a hairy, stinking man. This was fashion's power, after all. To disguise our most hideous weaknesses" (51). Dress and fashion have been indicators of one's degree, status, and wealth since Elizabethan sumptuary laws, and Boyet's observations about the ways in which clothing can disguise and create identity become ironic because they are true and not true. While fashion depends on performativity, masquerade, and disguise, the novel shows the limits of their powers. In detention, Boyet finds that nothing, not even cutting off the sleeves, can change the "Day-Glo orange" prison uniform (76). Clothing's power to disguise works only if one is not trapped by essentialist racial and gendered categories. Boyet is perceived to be gay because of his size and build, and because of his color and association with Ahmed he is mistaken for a terrorist regardless of how well connected or how well dressed he is.

Postmodern devices heighten the novel's uncertainty and surrealist quality. These devices include the insertion of extratextual materials, such as a magazine articles, footnotes, and nonfictional names. An article by fictional fashion reporter Gil Johannessen, titled "The Fall of (B)OY" (185), praises Boyet as a "budding designer" and compares his label "(B)oy" to American labels "Plaque, Urbane, Jeffrey Milk" (185). Another device is the use of deleted words in the narrative. Boy's confession contains words that have been redacted and footnotes explaining terms he uses. For example, a footnote explains, "habeas corpus, the writ by which detainees may seek relief from illegal imprisonment. This would challenge the legality of Boy's detention, though the Military Commissions Act (MCA), signed into law by the president on October 17, 2006, suspended habeas corpus for any alien determined to be an unlawful enemy combatant" (191). Historical characters populate the novel alongside fictive ones. When interrogators in Newark ask Boy about whom he knows, the list includes fictional and actual names: "Osama bin Laden, Khalid Sheikh Mohammed, Aman al-Zawahiri, George W. Bush, Dick Cheney, Ahmed Qureshi, Habib 'Hajji' Naseer, Michael Jordan, Mickey Mouse, Ben Laden, Philip Tang, Michelle Brewbaker, etc." (267).

As Boy writes about himself in his "confession," his life becomes more like a story, and he feels like a character in it. He notes, "Because everything I write about is in the past, I don't see myself as living anymore. This is what happens to you when you are arrested. The present is shifted instantly into the past, and what had once seemed unfathomable—torment, misery, profound suffering—is now actual" (267). He says, "Now that I approach the end of my confession, I find that I am beginning to lose hold of my character. I have become removed from the hero of my own story, you see. To lose hold of your own character must be part of the natural order of things in No Man's Land" (268). The afterword, ostensibly written by fashion reporter Gil Johannessen, seems more factual than Boyet's memoirs. It gives details about Boyet's unrecorded transfer to the nearby Camp No, "a solitary facility designed to break prisoners" (283), where he was isolated but "kept awake by the screams of other prisoners," who sounded as if they "were being severely tortured" or as if women were "being raped and beaten" (283). The sounds were "simulations intended to break prisoners" (283), and prisoner interrogations lasted for several consecutive days. After seven days at Camp No, Boyet is transferred to Camp Echo, "a holding facility for prisoners who were scheduled to meet with their lawyers," where he tries unsuccessfully to "take his own life" "using his towel and strips of cloth from a white undershirt" (285). Although a tribunal cannot find any "credible information" to link Boyet to terrorist groups (289), his six-month imprisonment and ordeal have ruined his aspirations to be a New York fashion designer. He is returned to the Philippines and becomes a shadow of what he once was, dressing as a woman to avoid being followed. His stay in America is an evanescent memory.

These postmodern devices highlight the difficulty of discerning the truth of information reported to us post-9/11. Authorities in the book claim, on the basis of Ahmed Qureshi's supposed declaration, that Boyet was the master financier of the terrorist plan. Boyet begins to feel as unreal as a character in a story. Historiographic metafiction suggests that "there are only *truths* in the plural, and never one Truth; and there is rarely falseness *per se*, just others' truths. . . . The interaction of the historiographic and the metafictional foregrounds the rejection of the claims of both 'authentic' representation and 'inauthentic' copy alike, and the very meaning of artistic originality is as forcefully challenged as is the transparency of historical referentiality" (Hutcheon, *Poetics* 109–10). Gilvarry's novel, partly in the form of a fictional memoir, is about failures of various sorts, including of the American dream. After 9/11, conceptions of race and gender became more rigid. Conceptions of masculinity narrowed rather than expanded, resulting in the typecasting of the hero, who was neither macho nor gay. The novel mocks how race and religion were conflated into a new category of "Middle Eastern" or brown, which could include Arabic, Muslim, South Asian, and Southeast Asian peoples or anyone with brown or dark skin. It is also a meditation on the absurdity of the popular media, the culture, and the arts industry, which is more interested in the fashionable, glitzy world of celebrities than in messy racial politics.

Ugly Feelings and Representational Strategies in *Tina's Mouth*

Keshni Kashyap and Mari Araki's graphic narrative *Tina's Mouth*, written in the form of a schoolgirl's diary addressed to French philosopher Jean Paul Sartre, follows the tribulations of an Indian American teen growing up in Southern California. The problems that beset fifteen-year-old Tina Malhotra are much less serious than those depicted in Gilvarry's novel. They include her estrangement from her best friend, whom she has known since fourth grade; her desire to acquire more grown-up "experience"; her crush on the popular skateboarder Neil Strumminger; and dealing with her well-meaning but impractical Indian family. Her struggle to find how she "fits into the world" is reminiscent of "any number of disaffected teens," as reviewers note (Kirkus Review), but what is different about this coming-of-age narrative is the unsentimental and quirky treatment of culture clashes and immigrant situations, as well as the unusual style of illustrations. These original representations and ways of telling a story may, in part, be due to Kashyap's training as a filmmaker and Araki's as a surrealist painter (Shah), but they also reflect the book's overarching theme of freedom.

In this section, I examine Kashyap and Araki's innovative narrative and representational techniques in *Tina's Mouth*, focusing on the book's rejection of comics' traditional division of pages into panels and frames (McCloud chap. 1). In addition, Araki's deliberately race-neutral and childlike illustrations present visual challenges to conventional representations of racial difference. I also look at intertextual references, such as Jean Paul Sartre's philosophy of existentialism, which provides a fitting backdrop to Tina's search for identity and authenticity. In conveying disenchantment with her parents and with friends who reject or don't understand her, Tina expresses what Sianne Ngai has called "ugly feelings," those "dysphoric or experientially negative" feelings, such as envy, that evoke pain or displeasure (11). Ngai argues that it is important to look not only at "scenes of high drama" but also at "moments of conspicuous inactivity" because they, too, are "affectively charged" (14). She suggests that "this feeling of confusion *about* what one is feeling"—what Tina experiences—is "an affective state in its own right" and "often heralds the basic affect of 'interest' underwriting all acts of intellectual inquiry" (14). Calling attention to how these ugly feelings arise can be a way of understanding the social institutions and collective practices that underlie our familial, gendered, social, and political lives.

Using illustrations that combine simple childish drawings and ornate decorations, Mari Araki gives us a sense of the protagonist's young age. Usually, backgrounds are understated, so the primary focus is on characters and their thoughts and experiences. Right at the outset, we are made aware of the juxtaposition between the bourgeoning adult and the child, between Tina's deep thinking and frivolousness, through Tina's obsession with Sartre, who is the inspiration for her Honors English project. Having been introduced in class to Sartre's idea that "life has no meaning beyond the goals that man sets for himself" (Kashyap and Araki 30), Tina likes Sartre so much that she clips his picture out of a book and tapes it to the wall above her bed along with a photo of her grandmother and other interesting artifacts, like a bug (31). This wall collection sets the lighthearted tone of the book and reveals the young protagonist to be quirky and romantic but intellectually curious and philosophical. What follows is the working out of the tensions between her various developing subjectivities.

The way Tina's family members are introduced is suggestive of their characters. Her family is shown initially as a photograph, where Tina stands a little bit away from her parents and two older siblings (11). At first glance, there is little indication that the family of five is Indian American—they are all wearing Western clothing—but the pictures behind the family are of an elephant and the Hindu god Krishna. In the next pages, the details of her parents' immigration thirty years ago are given simply in a two-page spread with maps, arrows indicating travel, and portraits of her parents in gilded frames (12–13). As in a number of twenty-first-century second-generation Asian American novels and films, including the previously discussed *Skim*, *The Debut*, and *Red Doors*, the story of displacement and immigration seems to be solidly in the past. The novel concerns itself less with arrival, struggle, and assimilation than with the protagonist's present-day adolescent concerns. It is her story of growing up—wishing for love, romance, and intellectual fulfillment. There are subtle differences in the ways the family members are introduced. Tina's parents are presented as photographs, with solid gilded frames around their pictures—a presentation that suggests stasis—while Tina's twenty-four-year-old sister, Anjali, is presented in action. Anjali is encircled by a vine with a small opening that suggests room for change and development. Anjali's artistic endeavours are summed up humorosly in a strip of black-and-white curves suggesting female bodies, called "Bodies" (14), and her lecture in New York in a speech bubble,

FIGURE 5. Tina as Alien

"Blah, blah, postcolonial, blah, blah, blah, hegemony, blah, diaspora, blah" (14). Her brother Rahul, who is twenty-eight, is framed with a solid square box, with a note that informs us that he can be a "pentagon" on the weekend, but "mostly he's a square" (15). The depictions of these family members within frames contrast with the depiction of Tina on a double page with psychedelic black-and-white lines emanating from her head. Making two horns with her hands, she says, "I'm an Alien . . . but my parents are Indian" (18–19).

The struggle in the book is not primarily about racial difference but about the search for self within an increasingly diverse community. It is an example of twenty-first-century works by Asian Americans that no longer are solely concerned about race as primary indications of their identity or as a basis for conflict. What is interesting about *Tina's Mouth* is the different ways the three siblings in the Malhotra family deal with their Indian American heritage. At the beginning of the novel, the eldest, Rahul, has seemingly followed the "model minority" route: he is in medical school studying to be a "cardio-something surgeon," according to Tina (15). He spends his time on an "Indian dating website" trying to find a girlfriend (15). Anjali, a product of Asian American studies, is a good postcolonialist, feminist artist, and critic. Her art exhibition ostensibly exposes the exploitation of women's bodies. Her lecture, involving the keywords *postcolonial*, *hegemony*, and *diaspora*, suggests leftist leanings—critical alliances with cultural

FIGURE 6. Tina's sister, Anjali

and Marxist theorists. Tina's response to racial difference is irritation, one of the feelings in Ngai's list of ugly feelings. These highly particularized feelings, such as "envy, irritation, anxiety, . . . paranoia, and disgust" (32), are different from strongly intentional emotions, such as jealousy, anger, and fear (20). Ngai notes that "ugly feelings can be described as conducive to producing ironic distance in a way that the grander and more prestigious passions, or even the moral emotions associated with sentimental literature, do not" (10).

One example of Tina's irritation appears when Tina talks about the questions she most frequently gets from strangers. These include "What's a good Indian restaurant?" and "What does the dot mean?" (Kashyap and Araki 20). Other questions are written in various fonts and scripts to form a circle, suggesting the dizzying effect such questions can have on Indian Americans. These typical questions come from individuals who can seemingly relate to an Asian American subject only as exotic or as a cultural Other. They range from general ones, like "Why is the cow sacred?," to personal ones, like "Are you going to have a dowry?" (21). The illustration suggests that the questions are overwhelming and can make Tina feel small but defiant. Though she does not comment on the questions, Araki draws her holding up her middle finger in response. Ngai suggests that negative affects such as irritation, though "amoral and noncathartic" (6), have "a remarkable capacity for duration" (7) and "[foreground] a failure of emotional release" (9). Though these feelings are not powerful ones that motivate action, they are constantly there, just below the surface. They can lead to ambivalence and irony, sometimes revealing one's resignation or pessimism, but Ngai believes that they can provide "critical productivity" (2–3). Tina does feel irritation and mild resentment at the way she is seen as Other, but she is also able to make use of her difference in a positive way. Her teacher, Mr. Moosewood, approaches her because he "just loves India," so he constantly finds occasions to talk to Tina about India (Kashyap and Araki 64). His encouragement leads her to get busy and "curtail [her] existential solitude" (66). Her reaction shows that she has accepted her exoticism and people's perception of her, but she is also not averse to taking some advantage of their Othering.

Tina lets Neil, the boy she thinks she is in love with, believe that she is familiar with Eastern religions. On their bike outing, he asks her about "nirvana," and she plays along with his notion that she is somehow knowledgeable about Buddhism. She thinks to herself, "I had some vague idea that nirvana had something to do with love and the universe and some kind of New Age nonsense that Mr. Moosewood would probably love. Or that it was something like that mysterious expanse Urvashi Auntie was talking about. I didn't know" (128). But she quickly makes up an answer that would lead to her goal of kissing Neil. Staring at his mouth, she tells him that Nivana has to do with the mouth. It turns out to be a "genius answer" (129) that leads to her long-awaited kiss of bliss (130). In a two-page spread, many wavy lines emanate from a mouth, suggesting her passionate feelings (130–31). For Tina, the kiss is both romantic, as shown by the flowers, hearts, and butterflies, and also exciting and explosive, as shown by the rocketship that blasts off. The conversation shows how she is able to take a stereotype and turn it around to her advantage. Tina's resolution to help herself, to get herself out of despondency and loneliness, is also due to the influence of existentialism. As her friend Hollis McAdams explains, "Sartre says that we aren't subject to fate . . . you make decisions based on who you are," but "there are consequences to everything we do" (69). This attitude marks a shift away from a discourse of passivity and victimhood to one of activity and responsibility, albeit sometimes in a humorous way.

Significantly, this kiss scene is located in the middle rather than at the end of the book. For while Tina tells us right from the start that she is obsessed with her mouth, and mouths, because "they speak, they taste, they sing," and most importantly, "it kisses" (27), repeatedly the novel questions ideals of Hollywood romance and falling in love. At first, Tina feels envious of all her friends who are part of romantic couples: she sees that Neil is dating Ava Petropoulos, who drives a Porsche (29); her best friend, Alex, starts dating a senior named

Eric and tells Tina that she is moving along to new experiences and doesn't want to hang around with her anymore (38, 43); and even her brother gets engaged to someone he met online (116). Tina's long-awaited first kiss turns out to be not with a boy she likes but with the creep Ted, who plays the male lead in the school play opposite Tina. Instead of a romantic kiss, she notes that "he plunged his bacteria-covered idiot savant tongue into my mouth and held it there for a good, long while" (111). However, within the space of a few weeks, things change. Neil's girlfriend Ava starts dating another boy, and Tina begins to imagine her future with Neil. When Neil asks her to go on a biking trip, all her fantasies about love and romance seem to be coming true (124), suggested by a two-page illustration of their bike trip. The illustration shows many hearts coming out of Tina's body during the bike ride, and this "magical day" culminates with the kiss (133). Tina believes that she is in love, but after the excursion, there is no declaration of love from Neil. Instead, while Neil continues to be friendly, she hears nothing more than casual remarks from him. Tina questions, "Could it be that my version of our bike ride and his version of the bike ride were two different things altogether?" (166). Alas, the kiss is not the prelude to everlasting romance.

Neil and Tina, it turns out, have different views about dating. Neil sees Tina as his "Buddhist biking buddy" but goes to a bedroom with her friend Hollis at a party, later calling it only a "drunk hook up" (205). The novel debunks illusions of romantic love as represented in the media and popular culture, because almost all the couples do not end up in a happily-ever-after state. Tina learns that her ex–best friend, Alex, has broken off with her boyfriend; her brother has a panic attack before his wedding, so he and his girlfriend decide to have a "disengaged" party instead of a wedding (216). Most importantly, Tina gets over Neil by throwing herself into her acting. The play, *Rashomon*, sells out and turns out to be a hit. Tina reflects, "I've been told that I have great potential as an actress. But for now, I'm just happy the whole semester is done. And that this whole kiss business is behind me" (210). The novel ends with her friendship, and possible budding romance, with their family friend, Reza, who is "very quiet" but who enjoys having "highly intellectual conversations" with her (68).

The *Rashomon* play provides an interesting intertexual commentary on Tina's life. The film on which it is based, a 1950 Japanese period drama directed by Akira Kurosawa, tells the story of a rape and murder scene from the perspective of various characters: a bandit, a dead samurai who speaks through a medium, the samurai's wife, and a woodcutter. Each character tells the story slightly differently at court, and the film questions the ways in which accounts of events can contain conflicting information. Tina's account of her friendships, love, and tribulations as a tenth-grade student, though not as serious as the events of *Rashomon*, is similarly subjective and perhaps illusory. As she concludes after talking to her friend about why Neil behaves the way he does with different girls, "There are, indeed, different but plausible versions of the truth" (163). The juxtaposition of the philosophical line with teen angst and puppy love helps create the work's irony and humor.

One problem is that Tina gets advice from her family that she cannot follow. When Tina's aunt fails to get Anjali paired up with a suitable match because Anjali is just not interested in the young doctor, her father tells them, "to thine own self be true" (153). Similarly, she receives contradictory advice from her feminist honorary aunt Urvashi: "I hope you are a feminist, darling, but don't be too much of one and never, ever become a lawyer, as you will work and work and work . . . in this idiotic country of yours and end up like one of those women on all those single women TV shows" (79). In her drunken state, Urvashi Auntie also tells her, "Be true to yourself," but then she says, "marry a European" (82–83). However, for Tina, the difficulty is that she does know what one thing she is. She says, "I will never be one thing. I am east, west, happy, sad, normal, freakish, plain, pretty, Indian, American and quite possibly a touch of Greek" (156). Later, when Reza asks who she is, Tina says, "I'm a lot of things . . . multifaceted" (228).

This refusal to be pinned down to just one thing, to follow the crowd, to do what is expected by her parents, is ultimately why Tina is able to conclude optimistically that her life is only beginning (240).

One interesting aspect of *Tina's Mouth* is Araki's way of representing South Asians in the novel. Araki has chosen not to give Tina, her family, and their Indian friends any shading to show difference from other characters in skin tones or hair color. Everyone is represented without color in the book. Derek Royal notes that graphic narratives always have a "problematic relationship to ethnic difference" because of their "reliance on character iconography" (8, 9). Royal argues that graphic narratives "can dismantle those . . . assumptions that problematize ethnic representation . . . by particularizing the general, thereby undermining any attempts at subjective erasure through universalization" (9). Following Scott McCloud, Royal believes that "[g]raphic narrative, in allowing the reader to 'mask' him- or herself in its non-mimetic figuration, invites empathy with the nondescript 'Other' on the comic page, thereby encouraging the reader to connect to other experiences and other communities that might otherwise have been unfamiliar" (10). In *Tina's Mouth*, Indianness is evident only through an occasional sari worn by her grandmother or one of the aunts. It is only at the end that Tina explicitly expresses an interest in something Indian, a plug-in Krishna, which is more cute or kitsch than religious. The effect of the drawings is somewhat jarring, but it makes readers aware of our visual expectations and reveals how conventional markers of racialized identity have structured our reading habits.

Tina's Mouth refuses to follow the usual racial or ethnic visual and thematic markers and shows that it is possible for an Asian American work to go beyond the usual topics of immigration, racial exclusion, and difference. Tina's ethnic heritage is only one of many concerns of this teen growing up in southern California. In the end, her ugly feelings of envy and irritation, and her confusion about her desires, her goals, and her identity, are not necessarily resolved, but they contribute to her assertion that although she is only sixteen, she has already understood what constructivist and poststructuralist theorists would call struggling with multiple and conflicted subjectivity. Unlike Boyet in Gilvarry's novel, Tina did not have to undergo detention and torture to figure out that who and what she is, is not what others expected.

Coda

In the increasingly diverse and growing Asian American population, the chance of getting a psychiatric disorder, including depression, is estimated at 17.3 percent. While the rate is lower than the rates of other minorities, the cultural stigma around treatment, and the barriers to getting it, concerns public health officials (Kam). Mental health is still an unaddressed issue, still often seen in Asian American families as a sign of weakness. In recent years, there have been serious attempts to make the public more aware of mental illness and to dissociate it from other affects, like shame and guilt. In the United States and Canada, government officials, mental health professionals, and community leaders are working together to address mental illness and suicide among Asian Americans and Pacific Islanders (see Kam; Centre for Research on Inner City Health). In Canada, the Canadian Mental Health Association provides fact sheets and details on how to find health services in Ontario on the web ("Help for Newcomers") and by phone. Bloggers and activists such as Jenn Fang from Reappropriate.co, a blog about Asian American culture and issues, have also written articles about the unreported high rates of depression and suicide in prominent U.S. universities and colleges. But more can and needs to be done.

In their own ways, the works I have studied in this book contribute to the growing awareness of the need to re-examine the "good life"—its high cost not only to youths but also to older members of the community, and its viability in the twenty-first century. Through inventive narrative and representational strategies that reveal precarious conditions, these works illuminate the critical social, cultural, historical, and political issues that most concern Asian North Americans in the twenty-first century. These issues, ranging from environmental degradation, the loss of stability from the financial crisis of 2007–8 and following, the suspicion and paranoia after 9/11, postwar trauma and memory, racialization and typecasting, and real and imagined cultural and familial expectations, mark the experiences of these artists I have studied. Between 2000 and 2015 the economic conditions in the United States and Canada have worsened due to the increasing neoliberal policies under the governments of Presidents Bill Clinton (1993–2001) and George W. Bush (2001–8) and of Prime Ministers Paul Martin (2003–6) and Stephen Harper (2006–15). American-model neoliberalism has been criticized because it results in "substantial levels of social exclusion, including high levels of income inequality, high relative and absolute poverty rates, poor and unequal educational outcomes, poor health outcomes, and high rates of crime incarceration" (Schmitt and Zipperer 15). For example, popular stances of both the U.S. and Canadian governments have been that we should be "tough on crime" and wage a "war on drugs." These notions resulted in an unprecedented rise of blacks and other minorities in U.S. prisons and of Aboriginal peoples in Canadian prisons. As Bruce Western notes, "Incarceration would be used less for rehabilitation than for incapacitation, deterrence, and punishment. . . . Tough new sentences were attached to narcotics offenses as the federal government waged first a war on crime, then a war on drugs. Locked facilities proliferated around the country to cope with the burgeoning penal population. Prison construction became an instrument for regional development as small towns lobbied for correctional facilities and resisted prison closure" (2–3).

Although these details do not directly relate to Asian North Americans, I argue that the movement from an ethic of care to the politics of the punitive, from rehabilitation to penal discipline, creates an atmosphere of fear, anxiety, and distrust in contemporary society. Only one of the texts in this study features incarceration of an Asian immigrant, but what is important is the institutional change, "shifts in the structure of society and politics" that have "large consequences for the quality of American democracy" (Western 2). If in the 1960s and early 1970s Asian American movements were formed in solidarity with and as a response to the Black Panther and Women's Liberation movements, then in the twenty-first century the criminalization of large numbers of young African Americans and First Nations Canadians has considerable effects on American and Canadian racial and social inequality, on the collective affective experiences of people of color and minorities. In the works I examined, we see the affect of fear in Vietnamese refugees who do not understand enough English to follow rules in *The Gangster We Are All Looking For*, or the dire consequences of the misrecognition of a Filipino immigrant in Gilvarry's *From the Memoirs of a*

Non-Enemy Combatant. The fear of the racial Other in the last decade has been exacerbated by the decline of manufacturing and industry and the dismantling of welfare state. It is not surprising that one of the most popular TV series in the last five or six years has been the American horror show *The Walking Dead* (2010–), where the fearful flesh-eating zombie Others turn out to be our own family members and neighbors rather than invaders from an external nation. People now fear contagion from those who are within rather than from strangers from a distant shore.

For this reason, it is heartening to see Asian Americans and Asian Canadians expressing solidarity with other disenfranchised groups and working for global environmental causes. The affiliations work to defy and counter the racially divisive idealization of Asian North Americans perpetuated by the model minority myth. For example, #Asians4Blacklives is a "diverse group of Asian voices coming from the Philippines, Vietnam, India, China, Pakistan, Korea, Burma, Japan, and other nations, based in the Bay Area," who "have come together in response to a call from Black Lives Matter Bay Area" to show solidarity with black people. The group recognizes that Asians, like blacks, are subjected to racism, misrecognition, and negative stereotyping. In her most recent book, *Undercurrent*, Asian Canadian poet Rita Wong vows to "honour what the flow of water teaches us" ("Declaration of Intent"), to be led by the "healing walkers" of the "Cree and Dene elders and everyday people" and to "reassert human responsibilities to land, water, life" ("Fresh Ancient Ground"). Wong stresses the need to form alliances with feminists and First Nations communities, recognizing that they will protect water and resist corporations that want to use the earth's resources as commodities.

Similarly, the Chinese Canadian Historical Society of BC is making a concerted effort to discover links between Chinese Canadians and First Nations people, producing videos called "Cedar and Bamboo" that highlight stories of marginalization by mixed-race Chinese/First Nations Canadians. The project goes beyond the history of Chinese immigrants in relationship to the gold rush, the building of the railroad, and Chinatowns to the historical and continuing relationships between the Chinese population and First Nations in British Columbia. Started by Chinese Canadian history professor Henry Yu, the online "Chinese Canadian Stories" feature information about key historical events in Chinese Canadian history as well as short videos made by university students about their background and issues that concern them. The project highlights the multiplicity of identities and ways of expressing these identities in the twenty-first century. One funny video that is a fine example of Asianfail is Jennifer Yip's "Hybrid Husband." The short video humorously depicts the pressure Yip feels at twenty-two to find a fiancé. Embarking on her twenty-seventh blind date to find the perfect Chinese/Canadian boyfriend, she meets a young man who seems to pass all the requirements set out by her family and herself. He speaks Cantonese and English, snowboards, skis, is learning to fly a plane, and understands her complicated hybrid culture. But by the end of the video, Yip is shocked and confounded by the discovery from his Facebook page that he already has a girlfriend. The video uses irony, humor, and exaggeration to cut through the tensions between a third-generation Asian Canadian and Old World cultural beliefs.

These instances I have been discussing here illustrate the increasing diversity of Asian North American subjects, and their responses to failure of various sorts. The works I have discussed show how Asian Americans and Asian Canadians are negotiating and reconfiguring their desires and aspirations. Although the works document different types of failure and depression, they also present alternatives to the current definitions of success, which center on professional and economic achievement. These novels, films, graphic narratives, and memoirs explore the consequences and rewards of not following or not being able to follow society's prescribed roads to success. As we have seen, the depicted reasons for failure include mental breakdown, shame, lingering memories of trauma and pain, the refusal to subscribe to capitalism's notion of success, and the rejection of the heteronormative romance script. Further failures are caused by bullying, misidentification and misrecognition, or the internalization of others' false assumptions and expectations. It is only through the telling of their stories that we understand the dystopic space in which many of these Asian North American people exist. They illuminate the precarity in the lives of some members of a group that has been perceived to be in a privileged space.

An inadvertent positive result of some members' failure to conform has been the production of an incredible assortment of works that question, in sometimes humorous, witty, ironic, and entertaining ways, our apprehension of our modern world, including our perception of the passing of time, of beauty, happiness, aging, gender, family life, and love. Sometimes, the failure to follow traditional routes leads to a new and unexpected way of finding peace and contentment, or an unexplored career path. In keeping with the motif of finding pleasures in the unpredictable, I deliberately sought to examine works that play with the conventions and forms of genre: the use of poetic prose, postmodern reiterations of Buddhist beliefs, stage performance with an inanimate character, a fake memoir, and a graphic narrative not contained by frames and sequences. This book is one of many efforts to participate in the ongoing and much-needed dialogue about priorities and values for our society, global environment, and political identities in the twenty-first century.

Works Cited

Filmography

American Beauty. Dir. Sam Mendes. Dreamworks, 1999.

Ararat. Dir. Atom Egoyan. Alliance Atlantis, 2002.

Charlotte Sometimes. Dir. Eric Byler. Hart Shop Video, 2002.

The Debut. Dir. Gene Cajayon. Sony Tristar, 2003.

Dirty Laundry. Prod. Richard Fung. 1996.

Double Happiness. Dir. Mina Shum. New Line Home Video, 1994.

Eat a Bowl of Tea. Dir. Wayne Wang. Columbia Tristar Home Video, 1989.

Educated. Dir. Georgia Lee. Written by Jane Chen and Georgia Lee. 2001. 11 min.

Exotica. Dir. Atom Egoyan. Miramax, 1994.

Family Viewing. Dir. Atom Egoyan. Cinephile. 1987.

Gran Torino. Dir. Clint Eastwood. Warner Bros. 2008.

Harold and Kumar Go to White Castle. Dir. Danny Leiner. Endgame Entertainment, 2004.

"Hybrid Husband." Dir. and played by Jennifer L. Yip. Prod. by INSTRCC. 3:55 min. Accessed 7 March 2016. http://ccs.library.ubc.ca/en/videos/instrcc_hybridhusband.html.

The Joy Luck Club. Dir. Wayne Wang. Buena Vista Home Video, 1993.

The Namesake. Dir. Mira Nair. Fox Searchlight, 2006.

Obaachan's Garden. Dir. Linda Ohama. National Film Board of Canada, 2001.

Red Doors. Dir. Georgia Lee. Polychrome Pictures, 2005.

Saving Face. Dir. Alice Wu. Sony Pictures Classics, 2004.

Shanghai Kiss. Dir. David Ren and Kern Konwiser. Starz Home Entertainment, 2007.

Speaking Parts. Dir. Atom Egoyan. Zeitgeist, 1990.

The Wedding Banquet. Dir. Ang Lee. Fox Video, 1993.

Who Killed Vincent Chin. Dir. Christine Choy and Renee Tajima. Film News Now Foundation, 1987.

Books, Articles, and Web Pages

A.G. "The Funny World of Fashion and Terrorism: The Q&A: Alex Gilvarry." *The Economist* 8 March 2012. Accessed 31 July 2014. http://www.economist.com/blogs/prospero/2012/03/qa-alex-gilvarry.

Administration on Aging. "A Statistical Profile of Asian Older Americans Aged 65+." *Administration for Community Living, U.S. Department of Health and Human Services*. n.d. Accessed 31 March 2015. http://www.aoa.acl.gov/Aging_Statistics/minority_aging/Facts-on-API-Elderly2008-plain_format.aspx.

Ahmed, Sara. "Collective Feelings: Or, the Impression Left by Others." *Theory, Culture, and Society* 21.2 (April 2004): 25–42.

———. *The Cultural Politics of Emotion*. 2004. New York: Routledge, 2010. Print.

———. *The Promise of Happiness*. Durham: Duke University Press, 2010. Print

American Psychological Association. "Suicide Among Asian-Americans." 2014. Accessed 9 May 2014. http://www.apa.org/.

Ang, Sze Wei. "The Politics of Victimization and the Model Minority." *CR: The New Centennial Review* 11.3 (2011): 119–40.

Appiah, Kwame Anthony. "Cosmopolitan Patriots." *Critical Inquiry* 23.3 (Spring 1997): 617–39.

Aquino, Francisca Reyes. "Singkil." *Folk Dances*. Vol 5. 1983. Excerpted in "Singkil." http://www.sinfonia.or.jp/~infortec/hotspots/boracay/singkil.htm.

"#Asian Fail." Accessed 20 December 2013. http://www.tumblr.com/tagged/asian-fail.

#Asians4Blacklives. Accessed 7 March 2016. https://a4bl.wordpress.com/.

Bal, Mieke, Jonathan Crewe, and Leo Spitzer, eds. *Acts of Memory: Cultural Recall in the Present*. Hanover, NH: Darmouth College Press / University Press of New England, 1998. Print.

Ball, David M. *False Starts: The Rhetoric of Failure and the Making of American Modernism, 1850–1950*. Evanston, IL: Northwestern University Press, 2014. Print.

———. "Toward an Archaeology of American Modernism: Reconsidering Prestige and Popularity in the American Renaissance." *ESQ: A Journal of the American Renaissance* ns 49.1–3 (2003): 161–77.

Barnes, Jessica, and Claudette E. Bennett. "The Asian Population: 2000: Census 2000 Brief." Collingdale, PA: Diane Publishing, 2000. 10 pp.

Bascara, Victor. *Model-Minority Imperialism*. Minneapolis: University of Minnesota Press, 2006. Print.

Bates, Judy Fong. *Midnight at the Dragon Café*. Toronto: McClelland and Stewart Emblem, 2004. Print.

Baudrillard, Jean. *The Spirit of Terrorism*. Trans. Chris Turner. London: Verso, 2002. Print.

Beiser, Morton, Feng Hou, Ilene Hyman, and Michel Tousignant. "Poverty, Family Process, and the Mental Health of Immigrant Children in Canada." *American Journal of Public Health* 92.2 (February 2002): 220–27.

Bell, David, and David G. Blanchflower. "Young People and Recession: A Lost Generation?" Paper Presented at the 52nd Economic Policy Panel Meeting, 22–23 October 2010.

Berlant, Lauren. *Cruel Optimism*. Durham: Duke University Press, 2011. Print.

Blake, Aaron. "The American Dream Is Hurting." *Washington Post* 24 September 2014. Accessed 7 February 2015. http://www.washingtonpost.com/blogs/the-fix/wp/2014/09/24/the-american-dream-is-hurting/.

Botz-Bornstein, Thorsten. "From the Stigmatized Tattoo to the Graffitied Body: Femininity in the Tattoo Renaissance." *Gender, Place and, Culture* 20.2 (2013): 236–52.

Brand, Dionne. *What We All Long For*. Toronto: Vintage Canada, 2005. Print.

Bulosan, Carlos. *America Is in the Heart*. 1943. Seattle: University of Washington Press, 1973. Print.

Butler, Judith. *Bodies That Matter: On the Discursive Limits of "Sex."* New York: Routledge, 1993. Print.

———. *Undoing Gender*. New York: Routledge, 2004. Print.

Canadian Mental Health Association. "Help for Newcomers." 2015. Acessed 27 May 2015. http://toronto.cmha.ca/mental_health/help-for-newcomers/#.VWcfCOd4hVQ.

Caruth, Cathy, ed. *Trauma: Explorations in Memory*. Baltimore: Johns Hopkins University Press, 1995. Print.

———. *Unclaimed Experience: Trauma, Narrative, and History*. Baltimore: Johns Hopkins University Press, 1996. Print.

Centre for Research on Inner City Health, Li Ka Shing Knowledge Institute, Keenan Research Centre, St. Michael's Hospital. "The Mental Health and Well-Being of Immigrants in Toronto: A Report to the Ministry of Health and Long-Term Care." March 2012. Toronto, ON.

Chambers-Letson, Joshua Takano. "Imprisonment/Internment/Detention." *The Routledge Companion to Asian American and Pacific Islander Literature*. Ed. Rachel C. Lee. London: Routledge, 2014. 144–53.

Chang, Mitchell J. "Expansion and Its Discontents: The Formation of Asian American Studies Programs in the 1990s." *Journal of Asian American Studies* 2.2 (June 1999): 181–206.

Chen, Suzette. "Jillian Tamaki and Mariko Tamaki." *Sequential Tart*. Accessed 11 February 2015. http://www.sequentialtart.com/archive/oct05/art_1005_3.shtml.

Cheng, Anne Anlin. *The Melancholy of Race: Psychoanalysis, Assimilation, and Hidden Grief*. New York: Oxford University Press, 2000. Print.

Cheuse, Alan. "All Things Considered: A First Novel that Pits the Far East with Canada." [Book Review of *Certainty*]. *NPR News*. 27 March 2007, 20:00–21:00 PM.

Chinese Canadian Historical Society. "Chinese Canadians and First Nations: 150 Years of Shared Experience." Accessed 7 March 2016. http://chinese-firstnations-relations.ca/.

Chinese Canadian Stories. 2012. Accessed 7 March 2016. http://ccs.library.ubc.ca/en/about.html.

Chiu, Monica, ed. *Drawing New Color Lines: Transnational Asian American Graphic Narratives*. Hong Kong: Hong Kong University Press, 2015. Print.

———. *Filthy Fictions: Asian American Literature by Women*. Walnut Creek, CA: Altamira, 2004. Print.

Chivers, Sally. *From Old Woman to Older Woman: Contemporary Culture and Women's Narratives*. Columbus: Ohio State University Press, 2003. Print.

Choi, Amy S. "The Angry Asian Man Is Actually a Really a Nice Guy." *The Mash Up Americans*. n.d. Accessed 29 February 2016. http://www.mashupamericans.com/issues/angry-asian-man-actually-really-nice-guy/.

Chong, Denise. *The Concubine's Children*. Toronto: Penguin, 1994. Print.

Chow, Rey. *The Protestant Ethnic and the Spirit of Capitalism*. New York: Columbia University Press, 2002. Print.

Choy, Wayson. *The Jade Peony*. Vancouver: Douglas and McIntyre, 1995. Print.

Chu, Louis. *Eat a Bowl of Tea*. 1961. Seattle: University of Washington Press, 1979. Print.

Chu, Patricia. *Assimilating Asians: Gendered Strategies of Authorship in Asian America*. Durham: Duke University Press, 2000. Print.

Chua, Amy. *Battle Hymn of the Tiger Mother*. New York: Penguin, 2011. Print.

———. "Battle Hymn of the Tiger Mom" web page. 2011. Accessed 7 January 2013. amychua.com.

Chua, Amy, and Jed Rubenfeld. *The Triple Package: How Three Unlikely Traits Explain the Rise and Fall of Cultural Groups in America*. New York: Penguin, 2014. Print.

Chuh, Kandice. *Imagine Otherwise: On Asian Americanist Critique*. Durham: Duke University Press, 2003. Print.

Chung, Angie Y. *Saving Face: The Emotional Costs of the Asian Immigrant Family Myth*. New Brunswick, NJ: Rutgers University Press, 2016. Print.

Clibbon, Jennifer. "Q&A: Jan Wong's Long March from Depression to Reinvention." *CBC News: Arts and Entertainment* 6 May 2012. Accessed 23 December 2013. www.cbc.ca/news/arts/.

Clifford, James. *Routes: Travel and Translation in the Late Twentieth Century*. Cambridge: Harvard University Press, 1997. Print.

Connor, Steven. *The Cambridge Companion to Postmodernism*. Cambridge: Cambridge University Press, 2004. Print.

Coser, Lewis. "Maurice Halbwachs, 1877–1945." Introduction. *On Collective Memory*. By Maurice Halbwachs. Chicago: University of Chicago Press, 1992. 1–34. Print.

Cover, Rob. "Becoming and Belonging: Performativity, Subjectivity, and the Cultural Purposes of Social Networking." *Identity Technologies: Constructing the Self Online*. Ed. Anna Poletti and Julie Rak. Madison: University of Wisconsin Press, 2014. 55–69. Print.

Cvetkovich, Ann. *Depression: A Public Feeling*. Durham: Duke University Press, 2012. Print.

Davis, Rocío. "Locating Family: Asian-Canadian Historical Revisioning in Linda Ohama's *Obaachan's Garden* and Ann Marie Fleming's *The Magical Life of Long Tack Sam*." *Journal of Canadian Studies* 42.1 (Winter 2008): 1–22. Project Muse. Retrieved 15 May 2011.

de Certeau, Michel. *The Practice of Everyday Life*. Trans. Steven Randall. Berkeley: University of California Press, 1988. Print.

DeLillo, Don. *Falling Man*. New York: Scribner, 2008. Print.

Dickerson, Mechele. "Is the American Dream Dead?" *The Conversation* 1 April 2016. Accessed 5 April 2016. https://theconversation.com/is-the-american-dream-dead-57095.

Edwards, Ivana. "The Essence of 'Kafkaesque.'" *New York Times* 29 December 1991. Accessed 5 November 2014. http://www.nytimes.com/1991/12/29/nyregion/the-essence-of-kafkaesque.html.

Espiritu, Yen Le. "Vietnamese Masculinities in lê thi diem thúy's *The Gangster We Are All Looking For*." *Revista Canaria de Estudios Ingleses* 66 (April 2013): 87–98.

Espiritu, Yen Le, and Thom Tran. "'Việt Nam, Nước Tôi' (Vietnam, My Country): Vietnamese Americans and Transnationalism." *The Changing Face of Home: Transnational Lives of the Second Generation*. Ed. Peggy Levitt and Mary C. Waters. New York: Russell Sage Foundation, 2002. 367–98. Print.

Faludi, Susan. *The Terror Dream: Fear and Fantasy in Post-9/11 America*. New York: Macmillan, 2007. Print.

Fang, Jenn. "Asian American Student Suicide Rate at MIT Is Quadruple the National Average." *Reappropriate* 20 May 2015. Accessed 25 May 2015. http://reappropriate.co/2015/05/asian-american-student-suicide-rate-at-mit-is-quadruple-the-national-average/.

Feng, Peter X. *Identities in Motion: Asian American Film and Video*. Durham: Duke University Press, 2002. Print.

Fischer, Michael. "Ethnicity and the Post-Modern Arts of Memory." *Writing Culture: The Poetics and Politics of Ethnography*. Ed. James Clifford and George Marcus. Berkeley: University of California Press, 1986. 194–215. Print.

Foer, Jonathan Safran. *Extremely Loud and Incredibly Close*. New York: Houghton Mifflin, 2005. Print.

Forster, E. M. *Howards End*. Harmondsworth: Penguin, 1977. Print.

Frankenberg, Ruth. *The Social Construction of Whiteness: White Women, Race Matters*. Minneapolis: University of Minnesota Press, 1993. Print.

Fraser, Nancy, and Linda J. Nicholson. "Social Criticism without Philosophy: An Encounter between Feminism and Postmodernism." *Feminism/Postmodernism*. Ed. Linda J. Nicholson. New York: Routledge, 1990. 19–38. Print.

Freud, Sigmund. *The Freud Reader*. Ed. Peter Gay. New York: Norton, 1989. Print.

Friedman, Susan Stanford. *Mappings: Feminism and the Cultural Geographies of Encounter*. Princeton: Princeton University Press, 1998. Print.

Fuckyeahnerdproblems. "Nerd Problem #41." Accessed 20 December 2013. http://fuckyeahnerdproblems-blog.tumblr.com/post/21412578082/submission-just-enough-to-be-disappointing.

Gilvarry, Alex. *From the Memoirs of a Non-Enemy Combatant*. New York: Viking, 2012. Print.

Goellnicht, Donald C. "A Long Labour: The Protracted Birth of Asian Canadian Literature." *Essays on Canadian Writing* 72 (Winter 2000): 1–41.

Gonzalez, Ed. Review of *Red Doors*. *Slant* 26 August 2006. Accessed 22 October 2010. Slantmagazine.com.

Government of Canada Labour Program. "Designated Group Profiles: 2006 Employment Equity Data Report." Released 2006 (Modified 2013-083-21). Accessed 19 February 2014. www.labour.gc.ca.

Greenfield Community College. "Writer—Le Thi Diem Thuy." Youtube Video. Uploaded 15 March 2010. Accessed 17 March 2015. https://www.youtube.com/watch?v=vIDbCTqCHMo.

Grewal, Inderpal. "Transnational America: Race, Gender, and Citizenship after 9/11." *Social Identities* 9.4 (2003): 535–61.

Halaby, Laila. *Once in a Promised Land*. Boston: Beacon, 2007. Print.

Halberstam, Judith. *The Queer Art of Failure*. Durham: Duke University Press, 2011. Print.

Halbwachs, Maurice. *On Collective Memory*. Ed. and trans. Lewis A. Coser. Chicago: University of Chicago Press, 1992. Print.

Hamamoto, Darrell Y. "The Joy Fuck Club: Prolegomenon to an Asian American Porno Practice." *CounterVisions: Asian American Film Criticism*. Ed. Darrell Y. Hamamoto and Sandra Liu. 59–89. Philadelphia: Temple University Press, 2000. Print.

Hamamoto, Darrell Y., and Sandra Liu, eds. *Countervisions: Asian American Film Criticism*. Philadelphia: Temple University Press, 2000. Print.

Hamid, Mohsin. *The Reluctant Fundamentalist*. Toronto: Anchor, 2008. Print.

Hardt, Michael. "What Affects Are Good For." Foreword. *The Affective Turn: Theorizing the Social*. Ed. Patricia Ticineto Clough with Jean Halley. Durham: Duke University Press, 2007. ix–xiii. Print.

Hashimoto, Akiko, and Charlotte Ikels. "Filial Piety in Changing Asian Societies." *The Cambridge Handbook of Age and Ageing*. Ed. Malcolm L. Johnson, in association with Vern L. Bengtson, Peter G. Coleman, and Thomas B. Kirkwood. Cambridge: Cambridge University Press, 2005. 437–42. Print.

Hattori, Tomo. "Model Minority Discourse and Asian American Jouis-Sense. *Differences: A Journal of Feminist Cultural Studies* 11.2 (Summer 1999): 228–47.

Hernandez, Catherine. *Eating with Lola*. Performance. FU-Gen Potluck Festival. Toronto, Factory Theatre, 8 May 2010.

———. *Eating with Lola*. Unpublished script. Dated 2010.

———. "Eating with Puppets." Blog. 11 May 2010. Accessed 29 July 2010. http://catherine hernandezwrites.blogspot.com/.

———. *Singkil*. Toronto: Playwrights Canada, 2009. Print.

Hirsch, Marianne. "The Generation of Postmemory." *Poetics Today* 29.2 (Spring 2008): 103–28. doi: 10.1215/03335372-2007-019

Ho, Khanh. "What Amy Chua Didn't Tell You: Why 'The Triple Package' Is Dead Wrong." *The Blog: Huffington Post* 14 February 2014. Accessed 30 April 2014. www.huffington post.com.

Holmlund, Chris. Introduction. *Contemporary American Independent Film: From the Margins to the Mainstream*. Ed. Chris Holmlund and Justin Wyatt. New York: Routledge, 2005. 1–16. Print.

Howie, Luke. *Terror on the Screen: Witnesses and the Reanimation of 9/11 as an Image Event.* Washington: New Academia, 2011. Print.

Huang, Betsy. "Popular Genres and New Media." *The Cambridge Companion to Asian American Literature.* Ed. Crystal Parikh and Daniel Kim. New York: Cambridge University Press, 2015. 142–54. Print.

Hutcheon, Linda. *Narcissistic Narrative: The Metafictional Paradox.* Waterloo, ON: Wilfrid Laurier University Press, 1980. Print.

———. *A Poetics of Postmodernism: History, Theory, Fiction.* New York: Routledge, 1988. Print.

———. *The Politics of Postmodernism.* New York: Routledge, 1989. Print.

Huyssen, Andreas. "Present Pasts: Media, Politics, Amnesia." *Globalization.* Ed. Arjun Appadurai. Durham: Duke University Press, 2001. 57–77. Print.

Igartua, Karine, Kathryn Gill, and Richard Montoro. "Internalized Homophobia: A Factor in Depression, Anxiety, and Suicide in the Gay and Lesbian Population." *Canadian Journal of Community Mental Health* 22.2 (2003): 15–30.

"Interview with Jan Wong." *CBC Strombo.* Accessed 6 June 2012. www.strombo.com.

Kam, Katherine. "Asian-Americans Tackle Mental Health Stigma." *WebMD Health News* 19 February 2015. Accessed 27 May 2015. http://www.webmd.com/mental-health/news/20150212/asian-americans-mental-health.

Kang, M. J. *Noran Bang: The Yellow Room.* 1993. *Love + Relasianships: A Collection of Contemporary Asian-Canadian Drama.* Vol. 1. Ed. Nina Lee Aquino. Toronto: Playwrights Canada, 2009. 191–236. Print.

Kaplan, Amy. "Manifest Domesticity." *American Literature* 70.3 (September 1998): 581–606.

Karpinski, Eva C. *Borrowed Tongues: Life Writing, Migration, and Translation.* Waterloo, ON: Wilfrid Laurier University Press, 2012. Print.

Kashyap, Keshni, and Mari Araki. *Tina's Mouth: An Existential Comic Diary.* New York: Houghton Mifflin, 2011. Print.

Kelly, Philip, Stella Park, Conely de Leon, and Jeff Priest. "Profile of Live-in Caregiver Immigrants to Canada, 1993–2009." *TIEDI: Toronto Immigrant Employment Data Initiative.* March 2011. Accessed 9 May 2014. www.yorku.ca/tiedi/doc.

Kembhavi, Rohan. "Canadian Seniors: A Demographic Profile." *Elections Canada* November 2012. Accessed 31 March 2015. http://www.elections.ca/res/rec/part/sen/pdf/sen_e.pdf.

Kimmel, Michael. *Misframing Men: The Politics of Contemporary Masculinities.* New Brunswick, NJ: Rutgers University Press, 2010. Print.

Kingston, Anne. "Jan Wong Dishes on Depression in the Workplace." *Macleans* 7 May 2012. Accessed 2 August 2013. www.macleans.ca.

Kingston, Maxine Hong. *The Woman Warrior: Memoirs of a Girlhood among Ghosts.* 1975. New York: Vintage, 1977. Print.

Kireev, Alex. "USA Presidential Elections 2008." *Electoral Geography 2.0: Mapped Politics.* 2007. http://www.electoralgeography.com/new/en/countries/u/usa/usa-presidential-election-2008.html.

Kirkus Review. *Tina's Mouth. Kirkus Review* 1 December 2011. Accessed 16 August 2014. https://www.kirkusreviews.com/book-reviews/keshni-kashyap/tinas-mouth/.

Kolbert, Elizabeth. "America's Top Parent: What's behind the 'Tiger Mother' Craze?" *New Yorker* 31 January 2011. Accessed 12 February 2014. www.newyorker.com/arts/critics/books.

Kong, Belinda. "The Asian-American Hyphen Goes Gothic: Ghosts and Doubles in Maxine Hong Kingston and lê thi diem thúy." *Asian Gothic: Essays on Literature, Film, and Anime.* Ed. Andrew Hock Soon Ng. Jefferson, NC: McFarland, 2008. 123–39. Print.

Koshy, Susan. "Neoliberal Family Matters." *American Literary History* 25.2 (2013): 344–80. doi: 10.1093/alh/ajt006.

Lai, Larissa. *Salt Fish Girl.* Toronto: Thomas Allen, 2002. Print.

———. *When Fox Is a Thousand.* Vancouver: Press Gang, 1995. Print.

Landsberg, Alison. *Prosthetic Memory: The Transformation of American Remembrance in the Age of Mass Culture.* New York: Columbia University Press, 2004. Print.

Lau, Evelyn. *Runaway: Diary of a Street Kid.* Toronto: HarperCollins, 1989. Print.

lê thi diem thúy. *The Gangster We Are All Looking For.* New York: Random Anchor, 2004. Print.

Lee, Georgia. "Director's Statement." 21 February 2007. Accessed 6 June 2010. http://www.reddoorsthemovie.com/.

Lee, Jennifer, and Min Zhou, eds. *Asian American Youth: Culture, Identity, and Ethnicity.* New York: Routledge, 2004. Print.

Lee, Josephine Tsui Yueh. *New York City's Chinese Community.* Charleston, SC: Arcadia, 2007. Print.

Lee, Rachel C. *The Exquisite Corpse of Asian America: Biopolitics, Biosociality, and Posthuman Ecologies.* New York: New York University Press, 2014. Print.

Lee, Sky. *Disappearing Moon Café.* Vancouver: Douglas and McIntyre, 1990. Print.

Lee, Stacey. "Additional Complexities: Social Class, Ethnicity, Generation, and Gender in Asian American Student Experiences." *Race Ethnicity and Education* 9.1 (March 2006): 17–28. doi: 10.1080/13613320500490630.

Li, Guofang. "Other People's Success: Impact of the 'Model Minority' Myth on Underachieving Asian Students in North America." *KEDI (Korean Educational Development Institute) Journal of Educational Policy* 2.1 (2005): 69–86.

Li, Peter S. *Chinese in Canada.* 2nd ed. Toronto: Oxford University Press, 1998. Print.

Lowe, Lisa. "Heterogeneity, Hybridity, Multiplicity: Marking Asian American Difference." *Diaspora* 1.1 (1991): 24–43. Print.

Mandiberg, Michael, ed. *The Social Media Reader.* New York: New York University Press, 2012. Print.

Marchetti, Gina. *Romance and the Yellow Peril: Race, Sex, and Discursive Hollywood Strategies in Hollywood Fiction.* Berkeley: University of California Press, 1993. Print.

Massumi, Brian. *Parables for the Virtual: Movement, Affect, Sensation.* Durham: Duke University Press, 2002. Print.

McCloud, Scott. *Making Comics.* New York: HarperCollins, 2006. Print.

McEwan, Ian. *Saturday*. Toronto: Vintage, 2006. Print.

McKittrick, Katherine. *Demonic Grounds: Black Women and the Cartographies of Struggle*. Minneapolis: University of Minnesota Press, 2006. Print.

McQueen, Paddy. "Social and Political Recognition." *Internet Encyclopedia of Philosophy*. Accessed 1 April 2016. http://www.iep.utm.edu/recog_sp/.

Messud, Claire. *The Emperor's Children*. Toronto: Vintage, 2007. Print.

Michael, Magali Cornier. "Don DeLillo's Falling Man: Countering Post-9/11 Narratives of Heroic Masculinity." *Portraying 9/11: Essays on Representations in Comics, Literature, Film, and Theatre*. Ed Véronique Bragard, Christophe Dony, and Warren Rosenberg. Jefferson, NC: McFarland, 2011. 73–88. Print.

Mimura, Glen M. *Ghostlife of Third Cinema: Asian American Film and Video*. Minneapolis: University of Minnesota Press, 2009. Print.

Moore, Charles. "Trashed: Across the Pacific Ocean, Plastics, Plastics Everywhere." *Natural History Magazine* 112.9 (November 2003). http://www.mindfully.org/Plastic/Ocean/Moore-Trashed-PacificNov03.htm.

Moore, Malcolm. "China's Precious Snowflakes: The Spoilt Children Who Never Lift a Finger." *Sydney Morning Herald* 9 January 2012.

Munro, Alice. *Lives of Girls and Women* (1971). Toronto: Vintage, 2001. Print.

Murphy, Edward F., Jr., Mark D. Woodhull, Bert Post, Carolyn Murphy-Post, William Teeple, and Kent Anderson. "9/11 Impact on Teenage Values." *Journal of Business Ethics* 69 (December 2006): 399–421.

Navaratnam, Sangeetha. "Guilt, Shame and Model Minorities: How South Asian Youth in Toronto Navigate the Canadian Educational System." Unpublished MA Thesis submitted to Sociology and Equity Studies, Ontario Institute for Studies in Education, 2011.

NAWHO (National Asian Women's Health Organization). "Empowering Avenues for Community Action: The National Collaborative for Asian American Women's Mental Health." Accessed 3 January 2014. www.nawho.org.

Ngai, Sianne. *Ugly Feelings*. Cambridge, MA: Harvard University Press, 2005. Print.

Nikkei National Museum and Cultural Centre. "Japanese Canadian Timeline." Accessed 30 April 2014. centre.nikkeiplace.org.

Ninh, erin Khuê. *Ingratitude: The Debt-Bound Daughter in Asian American Literature*. New York: New York University Press, 2011. Print.

Nishime, LeiLani. "'I'm Blackanese': Buddy-Cop Films, *Rush Hour*, and Asian American and African American Cross-Racial Identification." *Asian North American Identities Beyond the Hyphen*. Ed. Eleanor Ty and Donald C. Goellnicht. Bloomington: Indiana University Press, 2004. 43–61. Print.

Offman, Craif. "Tiger Mom Amy Chua's Theory of Success: Three Factors Why Indians, Jews, Chinese Do Better Than Others." *Globe and Mail* 5 February 2014. Accessed 30 April 2014. www.theglobeandmail.com.

Oliver, Kelly. *Witnessing: Beyond Recognition*. Minneapolis: University of Minnesota Press, 2001. Print.

Ondaatje, Michael. *In the Skin of a Lion*. 1987. Toronto: Vintage Canada, 1996. Print.

O'Neill, Joseph. *Netherland.* Toronto: Vintage, 2009. Print.

Osajima, Keith. "Asian Americans as the Model Minority: An Analysis of the Popular Press Image in the 1960s and the 1980s." *A Companion to Asian American Studies.* Ed. Kent A. Ono. Malden, MA: Blackwell, 2005. 215–25. Print.

Ozeki, Ruth. *All Over Creation.* New York: Penguin, 2003. Print.

———. *My Year of Meats.* New York: Viking, 1998. Print.

———. *A Tale for the Time Being.* New York: Viking, 2013. Print.

Palumbo-Liu, David. *Asian/American: Historical Crossings of a Racial Frontier.* Stanford: Stanford University Press, 1999. Print.

———. "Universalisms and Minority Culture." *Differences: A Journal of Feminist Cultural Studies* 7.1 (1995): 188–208. Print.

Perrucci, Robert, and Earl Wysong. *The New Class Society: Goodbye American Dream?* 3rd ed. Lanham, MD: Rowman and Littlefield, 2008. Print.

Polakow-Suransky, Sasha. "Flying While Brown." *American Prospect* 10 December 2001. prospect.org/article/flying-while-brown.

Ponce, Martin Joseph. *Beyond the Nation: Diasporic Filipino Literature and Queer Reading.* New York: New York University Press, 2012. Print.

Pratt, Geraldine. *Families Apart: Migrant Mothers and the Conflicts of Labor and Love.* Minneapolis: University of Minnesota Press, 2012. Print.

"Racial Profiling Cited as Writer Cancels U.S. Tour." *CBC News* 3 November 2002. www.cbc.ca/news/canada.

Rho, Yanni, and Kathy Rho. "Clinical Considerations When Working with Asian American Children and Adolescents." *Handbook of Mental Health and Acculturation in Asian American Families.* Ed. Nhi-Ha Trinh, Yanni Chun Rho, Francis G. Lu, and Kathy Marie Sanders. New York: Humana, 2009. 143–66. Print.

Rich, Adrienne. *Of Woman Born: Motherhood as Experience and Institution.* 1976. Tenth Anniversary Ed. New York: Norton, 1986. Print.

Roley, Brian. *American Son.* New York: Norton, 2001. Print.

Royal, Derek Parker. "Introduction: Coloring America: Multi-Ethnic Engagements with Graphic Narrative." *MELUS* 32.3 (Fall 2007): 7–22.

Rushdie, Salman. *The Ground beneath Her Feet.* 1999. Toronto: Vintage Canada, 2000. Print.

Safran, William. "Diasporas in Modern Societies: Myths of Homeland and Return." *Diaspora* 1 (Spring 1991): 83–99.

Saltman, Judith. Review of *Skim. Quill and Quire* March 2008. http://www.quillandquire.com/books_young/review.cfm?review_id=5989.

Santa Ana, Jeffrey. *Racial Feelings: Asian America in a Capitalist Culture of Emotion.* Philadelphia: Temple University Press, 2015. Print.

Scarry, Elaine. *The Body in Pain: The Making and Unmaking of the World.* New York: Oxford University Press, 1987. Print.

Schmitt, John, and Ben Zipperer. "Is the U.S. a Good Model for Reducing Social Exclusion in Europe?" *CEPR: Center for Economic and Policy Research: Reports* July 2006. 1–28. Accessed 25 February 2016. cepr.net/documents/social_exclusion_2006_08.pdf.

Scott, Alec. "Write of Passage: Madeleine Thien's Quest for *Certainty*." [Book Review] 5 June 2006. Accessed 11 October 2007. http://www.cbc.ca/arts/books/thien.html.

Seigworth, Gregory J., and Melissa Gregg. "An Inventory of Shimmers." *The Affect Theory Reader*. Ed. Melissa Gregg and Gregory J. Seigworth. Durham: Duke University Press, 2010. 1–25. Print.

Shah, Angilee. "*Tina's Mouth*: A Graphic Novel That Gives Indian-American Stereotypes the Finger." *LA Weekly Blogs* 31 January 2012. Accessed 16 August 2014. http://www.laweekly.com/publicspectacle/2012/01/31/tinas-mouth-a-graphic-novel-that-gives-indian-american-stereotypes-the-finger.

Shimizu, Celine Parreñas. *The Hypersexuality of Race: Performing Asian/American Women on Screen and Scene*. Durham: Duke University Press, 2007. Print.

Shouse, Eric. "Feeling, Emotion, Affect." *M/C Journal* 8.6 (December 2005). Retrieved 12 April 2011. http://journal.media-culture.org.au/0512/03-shouse.php.

Smith, Jon, and Deborah Cohn. "Uncanny Hybridities." Introduction. *Look Away! The U.S. South in New World Studies*. Ed. Jon Smith and Deborah Cohn. Durham: Duke University Press, 2004. 1–19. Print.

Smith, Sidonie, and Julia Watson. *Reading Autobiography: A Guide for Interpreting Life Narratives*. 2nd ed. Minneapolis: University of Minnesota Press, 2010. Print.

Smith, Zadie. *White Teeth*. London: Penguin, 2000. Print.

So, Jimmy. "Reading the Best 9/11 Novels." *Daily Beast* Books 11 September 2013. Accessed 1 August 2014. http://www.thedailybeast.com/articles/2013/09/11/reading-the-best-9-11-novels.html

Song, Min Hyoung. *The Children of 1965: On Writing, and Not Writing, as an Asian American*. Durham: Duke University Press, 2013. Print.

"State of Theatre: Catherine Hernandez." *BlogTO* 10 January 2007. Accessed 28 July 2010. http://www.blogto.com/theatre/2007/01/the_state_of_theatre_catherine_hernandez/.

Statistics Canada. "2011 National Household Survey: Immigration, Place of Birth, Citizenship, Ethnic Origin, Visible Minorities, Language and Religion." Released 8 May 2013. Accessed 19 February 2014. www.statcan.gc.ca.

———. "The Filipino Community in Canada." No. 5 (2007). http://www.statcan.gc.ca/pub/89-621-x/89-621-x2007005-eng.htm.

Steger, Manfred. *Globalization: A Very Short Introduction*. Oxford: Oxford University Press, 2003. Print.

Stephenson, Peter H. "Age and Time: Contesting the Paradigm of Loss in the Age of Novelty." *Contesting Aging and Time*. Ed. Janice E. Graham and Peter H. Stephenson. Toronto: University of Toronto Press, 2010. 3–25. Print.

Stewart, Susan. *On Longing: Narratives of the Miniature, the Gigantic, the Souvenir, the Collection*. Durham: Duke University Press, 1993. Print.

Sturken, Marita. "Absent Images of Memory: Remembering and Reenacting the Japanese Internment." *Perilous Memories: The Asia-Pacific War(s)*. Ed. T. Fujitani, Geoffrey White, and Lisa Yoneyama. Durham: Duke University Press, 2000. 33–49. Print.

Tamaki, Mariko. *Cover Me*. Toronto: McGilligan, 2000. Print.

Tamaki, Mariko, and Jillian Tamaki. *Skim*. Toronto: House of Anansi, 2008. Print.

Tan, Amy. *The Joy Luck Club*. New York: Ballantyne Ivy, 1989. Print.

Tayag, Michael. "Great Expectations: The Negative Consequences and Policy Implications of the Asian American 'Model Minority' Stereotype." *Standford Journal of Asian American Studies* 4.1 (Spring 2011): 23–31.

Taylor, Charles. "The Politics of Recognition." *Multiculturalism: Examining the Politics of Recognition*. Ed. Amy Gutmann. Princeton: Princeton University Press, 1994. 25–73. Print.

Thien, Madeleine. *Certainty*. Toronto: McClelland and Stewart, 2006. Print.

Thomson, Rosemarie. *Extraordinary Bodies: Figuring Disability in American Literature and Culture*. New York: Columbia University Press, 1996. Print.

Timson, Judith. "Are Our Pampered Kids under Too Much Pressure?" *Globe and Mail* 2 August 2012.

Toews, Miriam. *A Complicated Kindness*. Toronto: Vintage, 2007. Print.

Troeung, Y-Dang. "Forgetting Loss in Madeleine Thien's *Certainty*." *Canadian Literature* 206 (Autumn 2010): 91–108.

Ty, Eleanor. *The Politics of the Visible in Asian North American Narratives*. Toronto: University of Toronto Press, 2004. Print.

———. *Unfastened: Globality and Asian North American Narratives*. Minneapolis: University of Minnesota Press, 2010. Print.

Ty, Eleanor, and Donald C. Goellnicht, eds. *Asian North American Identities: Beyond the Hyphen*. Bloomington: Indiana University Press, 2004. Print.

U.S. Census Bureau. "Three-Year-Average Median Household Income by State: 2002–2004." 30 August 2005. Accessed 17 July 2011. http://www.census.gov/hhes/www/income/income04/statemhi.html.

U.S. News and World Report. "Success Story of One Minority Group in U.S." Reprinted. *Asian American Studies: A Reader*. Ed. Jean Yu-Wen Shen Wu and Min Song. New Brunswick, NJ: Rutgers University Press, 2000. 158–63. Print.

van der Kolk, Bessel, and Onno van der Hart. "The Intrusive Past: The Flexibility of Memory and the Engraving of Trauma." *Trauma: Explorations in Memory*. Ed Cathy Caruth. Baltimore: Johns Hopkins University Press, 1995. 158–82. Print.

Warn, Sarah. Review of *Red Doors*. *AfterEllen*. 1 May 2005. Accessed 13 August 2011. http://www.afterellen.com/movies/4192-review-of-red-doors.

Western, Bruce. *Punishment and Inequality in America*. New York: Russell Sage Foundation, 2006. Print.

Williams, Trish, Jennifer Connolly, Debra Pepler, and Wendy Craig. "Questioning and Sexual Minority Adolescents: High School Experiences of Bullying, Sexual Harassment, and Physical Abuse." *Canadian Journal of Community Mental Health* 22.2 (2003): 47–58.

Wolf, Diane L. "Family Secrets: Transnational Struggles among Children of Filipino Immigrants." *Sociological Perspectives* 40.3 (1997): 457–82.

Wong, Jade Snow. *Fifth Chinese Daughter*. New York: Harper, 1945. Print.

Wong, Jan. *Out of the Blue*. Canada: Jan Wong, 2012. Print.

Wong, Rita. *Undercurrent*. Gibsons, BC: Nightwood, 2015. Print.

Wong, Sau-ling Cynthia. "Ethnic Subject, Ethnic Sign, and the Difficulty of Rehabilitative Representation: Chinatown in Some Works of Chinese American Fiction." *Yearbook of English Studies: Ethnicity and Representation in American Literature* 24 (1994): 251–62. Print.

———. "'Sugar Sisterhood': Situating the Amy Tan Phenomenon." *The Ethnic Canon: Histories, Institutions, and Interventions.* Ed. David Palumbo-Liu. 174–210. Minneapolis: University of Minnesota Press, 1995. Print.

Woolf, Virginia. "A Sketch of the Past." *The Broadview Anthology of British Literature.* Concise Ed., Vol. B. Ed. Joseph Black et al. 1211–15. Peterborough, ON: Broadview, 2007. Print.

———. *To the Lighthouse.* Frogmore, St. Albans: Triad Panther, 1977. Print.

Xing, Jun. *Asian America Through the Lens: History, Representations, and Identity.* Walnut Creek, CA: Altamira, 1998. Print.

Yu, Phil. *Angry Asian Man.* Blog. Accessed 29 February 2016. http://blog.angryasianman.com/.

Zamir, Tzachi. "Puppets." *Critical Inquiry* 36.3 (Spring 2010): 386–409. JSTOR. Retrieved 27 May 2011. http://www.jstor.org/stable/10.1086/653406.

Index

ELEANOR TY is a professor of English and film studies at Wilfrid Laurier University in Ontario. She is the author of *Unfastened: Globality and Asian North American Narratives* and coeditor of *Canadian Literature and Cultural Memory*.

The University of Illinois Press
is a founding member of the
Association of American University Presses.

Cover designed by Jennifer S. Holzner
Cover illustration: Trinidad Escobar
(www.trinidadescobar.com)

University of Illinois Press
1325 South Oak Street
Champaign, IL 61820-6903
www.press.uillinois.edu